"By accident, or on purpose they shun the Church as one would a haunted house. To all appearances, and judging from this letter, millions of citizens in the United States know the Church only as a caricature, a deformity, a superstition, a haunted house."

This caricature of the Church has caused the Christian world to be divided into Catholic and Protestant. This monument of prejudice stands between them, blocking the path of peace and good will among men. It is my intention in the following pages to show in terms of fact, not in terms of fiction, that the Protestant world in America is in conflict not with the Catholic world, but with a caricature, a calumny, a deformity, which evil has invented and represented as the Church. If this can be proved to their utter satisfaction, we trust that the millions of hearts that stand apart will come nearer and discover that God made them all alike to love one another.

Without facts there can be no case!

D0992554

ROME
AND THE
WHITE HOUSE

THE VATICAN

THE CAPITOL

ROME
AND THE
WHITE HOUSE

POPE AND PRESIDENT

"A PARALLEL"

BY

JAMES A. HYLAND, C.S.Sp., M.A.

NEW YORK
THE DEVIN-ADAIR COMPANY

15326

COPYRIGHT, 1928, BY
THE DEVIN-ADAIR COMPANY

———

All Rights Reserved by
THE DEVIN-ADAIR COMPANY

CUM PERMISSU SUPERIORUM

Imprimatur:

✠ JULES B. JEANMARD,

Bishop of Lafayette.

Lafayette, Louisiana.   May 3, 1928

First Large Printing.....September, 1928
Second Large Printing......October, 1928

BR
516
H8

Printed in the United States of America

FOREWORD

This book treats of the most interesting person-
ages in the world: The Pope and the President. For
twenty centuries the Pope has been, in the spiritual
sphere, the most colorful figure of the Christian
world. In the civilized political world he has always been regarded as a foremost exponent of the
ethical law and the system of social relations between
states and nations: as a moral power above and
beyond the reach of material powers. To-day thirty-
five nations have representatives at the Vatican, and
the Powers not officially represented are always in
close touch with the Holy See.

G. K. Chesterton in an article on "Peace and the
Papacy," which appeared during 1928, said: "The
world will more and more find itself in a position,
in which even politicians and practical men will find
themselves saying: 'If the Pope had not existed it
would be necessary to invent him.' The truth is that
multitudes of them would already accept the Pope if
he were not called the Pope."

The President of the United States is indeed the
personal embodiment of a nation which we Americans believe is "the greatest country on earth." He
is the head of a government which we love to think

stands for what is best in the world. The history of
the Presidents of the United States tells a story of
the most perfect union and the most successful government ever organized among men.

What is the relation existing between these two
world figures, and between these two great governments, the one spiritual, the other civil? Do the subjects of each of these respective governments practice the Christian principle: "Render therefore unto
Cæsar the things that are Cæsar's, and to God, the
things that are God's?"

In this book the reader will find side by side in
parallel comment and illustration, the basic institutions of the Catholic Church and the United States.
Look them over carefully with your own eyes, and
see if they are in conflict.

For several years the writer has had a favorable
opportunity to be associated with Protestants and
non-Catholics in the Southland, to love and appreci-
ate them, and to learn their view-points. To his
amazement and often to his amusement he found
that what they fear and oppose is not the Catholic
Church, but something else which "the Protestant
Tradition" represented to them as the Church. They
fear an evil which does not exist.

The object of this work is to correct the existing
evil, "the Protestant Tradition," and show them the
real Catholic Church in its relation to the real
United States. The plain American people are fair-
minded; and when they discover that what they

were taught to despise is not the Church, but a hideous misrepresentation, intolerance will melt away before the rising sun of truth; PEACE AND LOVE WILL WALK HAND IN HAND.

THE AUTHOR.

Opelousas, Louisiana.

CONTENTS

LIST OF ILLUSTRATIONS

ROME

AND THE

WHITE HOUSE

"If a Catholic, no matter how worthy were now elected President of the United States, the prayers of millions of Protestants to Jesus were indeed in vain. This I will not admit! This is not the occasion to say let us forget the past. The past is part of the present and the pledge of the future.

"Stories of Catholic cruelty and intrigue have come down to us for two hundred years and more The Spanish Inquisition is not dead but sleepeth! It is waiting for a Catholic President to restore it in the United States. I cannot for the life of me understand why you enlightened men, for no one has ever accused you of ignorance, would not rise up and shake off this invention of Satan, this gigantic machine. Why not turn to the simple truths of Jesus: 'Learn of me and heed not those priestly incantations.' Oh, what would the world be without Jesus! I often wondered what tears must be shed in heaven as Jesus looks down on the earth filled with Catholic altars for the worship of false Gods—beads, Scapulars, cheap medals, holy water, signs and symbols!

"Time does not seem to erase from my brain this impression of your Church, and you, I am sure in your heart, must reject it too. But even should you tear yourself away from the spells and oriental magic of Rome, the position of Catholics remains the same. Your Cardinals preach: 'We are the same yesterday, today and forever.' If you are a practical citizen, it is in spite of your allegiance to Rome.

"Critics are amazed at the hypnotic effect of the whole machine on society; that it suggests the presence of something preternatural which charms the senses in order to steal away the reason of men. They even quote examples where the unthinking have fallen into its snares and incantations, and were destroyed. Even as our fathers told us, so do we find it. And as I grow older I realize the wisdom of our ancestors in Jesus: 'Fly whenever Rome's agents draw near.' The weight of this great Protestant tradition you cannot ignore.

"Nor do we see any relief in sight. For the Catholic Church seems forever to escape the fate which brings all other institutions into life, maturity, old age, decay and memory. Mind you, I do not question the learning, sagacity and prudence of your Cardinals and Popes. Their lieutenants, the Archbishops and Bishops stand alone, dominant and circled around by an aureola of intellectual superiority.

"All history recounts how tidal waves of bloody war, secret plottings, volcanic social eruptions, etc., have all alike failed to sweep the system of Rome into oblivion. The observation of the best historians is that for political prestige, national or international these men care nought. If they consider these little things it is for a pastime.

"The real objective of the whole system is nothing less than the control of the fundamental principles of human thought, in a word, they want the conscience of every man within the hollow of their

hands. They employ any means no matter how un-
worthy to bring about the destruction of Americanism and Protestantism. Documents are now coming
to light, and will be published in the near future,
which will implicate the Pope as the real founder
of the Ku Klux Klan, to bring discredit on Protestantism in America. Americanism and Catholicism
are as far apart as democracy and autocracy.

"I think I have proven [1] that the Roman Catholic
Church is founded on the principles of pagan superstition, which you yourself will admit are in open
conflict with the Christian and Protestant principles
of the Declaration and Constitution of the United
States. Can one conceive a loyal Catholic proving
himself a loyal American and still remain Catholic?
Can you conceive how a heathen may be a loyal
heathen and still be a loyal Christian? Can a thing
be black and white at the same time? I leave you
yourself and your good sense to answer. But however you get around these questions, Protestants deep
down in their hearts, believe that what was handed
down is true, that there is something indefinable
about the Catholic Church, to which the American
mind is inherently opposed."

Taking Shakespeare's suggestion, the writer of
this letter has essayed "to hold as 'twere the mirror

---

[1] The writer has fallen into the old error of presuming that
whatever is clear in his own mind is clear to all other minds. He
has not produced any acceptable proof of this assertion, and his
presumption of proof is not evidence.

up to nature; to show virtue her own feature, scorn her own image, and the very age and body of the time his form and pressure." Indeed Robert Burns must have ardently admired this gift when he wrote:

"O wad some Power the giftie gie us
To see oursels as ithers see us!"

If millions of Protestants see us in this picture, little wonder they do not like us! It is, rather, surprising they do not deport us to the Nile or the Dark Ages. But Americans are tolerant and fair-minded. They hate bigotry and whatever smacks of persecution toward the ignorant and unfortunate. Contempt usually begets pity. "Blessed are the merciful: for they shall obtain mercy." [2] The majority show their mercy and tolerance by shunning us. They fear the Church, not that they are afraid, but that it might "deprive their sovereignty of reason and draw them into madness" if they should

"Offer it the show of violence,
For it is as the air invulnerable,
And our vain blows malicious mockery." [3]

Therefore, by accident, or on purpose they shun the Church as one would a haunted house. To all appearances, and judging from this letter, millions of citizens in the United States know the Church only as a caricature, a deformity, a superstition, a haunted house.

[2] Matthew V. 7.
[3] Shakespeare: "Hamlet" Act I. Scene 1.

This they were told. The only reason they advance for their belief is tradition. They heard their fathers curse it. Therefore it is a thing accursed. Is their opinion of us sincere? No one can doubt that. This Protestant tradition is kept alive in Sunday-school stories, in novels, literature, histories; and the great tradition about Catholics is always sure of a respectable hearing. When we read history and see how consistently people have made fools of themselves in regard to the Catholic Church, we recall Mr. Barnum's observation in speaking of fools: "There is one born every minute." But worse than that, we begin to be ashamed of our human nature. Life indeed often seems to be a comedy of errors, a record of the world's fooleries and mistakes. The errors and wrongs of the twentieth century will be discovered in the twenty-second, and others made for future centuries to discover and correct. What was accepted as fact yesterday is fiction today, legend tomorrow and myth next day.

The lie seems to have a long life. Here in the United States, in spite of business relations, intermarriage and social friendships, the spirit of intolerance still lingers in the consciousness of many Protestants. And now in the time of a national election the ghost of prejudice rises from its grave, walks abroad and scares the wits out of credulous politicians, steals furtively into the lodge, and whispers: "Beware!" Have I not seen the man who heard a man say he saw the man who had seen the

ship on which the Pope intends to come to the United
States and enter the White House by the chimney?
"Beware!" [4] At first sedate men laugh at such fool-
ishness, but when the ghost keeps up wailing—
"beware!—beware!"—they begin to say to themselves: "Well, it is not impossible; after all, it agrees
with what we heard when we were young. The
Catholic Church is an anachronism in the United
States, and has no place in our young republic which
is 'free, white and twenty-one'."

This caricature of the Church has caused the
Christian world to be divided into Catholic and
Protestant. This monument of prejudice stands between them, blocking the path of peace and good
will among men. It is my intention in the following
pages to show in terms of fact, not in terms of fiction, that the Protestant world in America is in
conflict not with the Catholic world, but with a caricature, a calumny, a deformity, which evil has invented and represented as the Church. If this can
be proved to their utter satisfaction, we trust that
the millions of hearts that stand apart will come
nearer and discover that God made them all alike to
love one another.

Without facts there can be no case!

Now the two greatest institutions in the world

---

[4] These citizens overlook that the world was ages old, and the
Christian Religion was over 1700 years old at the time this new
Republic came into existence. Would any patriot suggest that
because we needed a new government, we also needed a new
religion?

today are the United States and the Catholic Church. The one is a human and the other a Divine institution. In 1926 two memorable gatherings took place in the United States: The Eucharistic Congress in Chicago; and the Sesquicentennial at Philadelphia. At these two meetings there passed in review the histories of these two institutions, the Church and the American Republic.

The Sesquicentennial at Philadelphia reviewed the trials and triumphs of our American Government since its birth one hundred and fifty years ago. The Eucharistic Congress pictured the unbroken unity of the Church from the first Pentecost down to the present time. That which keeps Catholic and Protestant citizens divided is the Protestant tradition: the belief that the institutions of the Church are in fact and principle in open conflict with those of the Government of the United States. Let us place side by side in parallel lines the fundamental institutions of the Church and those of the State, and see whence the conflict arises.

Facts cure suspicion!

II

CATHOLIC DECLARATION OF SPIRITUAL INDEPENDENCE

"Look into the Rock whence you are hewn."

(Isaias LI. 1.)

"And you shall know the truth, and the truth shall make you free." (St. John VIII. 32.)

BEHOLD now the Declaration of the Spiritual Independence of the Church! There is Christ the Founder in the midst of His Apostles. He is organizing a Divine Society. "I am come" He said, "that they may have life, and may have it more abundantly." [1] He restated those eternal truths of Heaven which, because of the tyranny of sin, had become dim and obscure in the hearts of men. He did not abolish old truths but confirmed and completed them in the New Law. Christ came when men had admitted failure. He came in answer to the cry: "Drop down dew, ye heavens, from above, and let the clouds rain the just: let the earth be opened, and bud forth a Savior: and let Justice spring up together." [2] He came to re-make and re-organize a society on the verge of destruction.

[1] John X. 10.
[2] Isaias XLV. 8.

The declaration of this New Law and its effects on civilization are beautifully set forth by that eminent scholar and historian, Dr. Godfrey Kurth, in his lecture WHAT ARE THE MIDDLE AGES? He says:

"There is a line of demarcation which separates into two grand divisions the history of humankind. It is the line which bears on its summit the Cross of Golgotha. And why? Because it is there that was heard the Fiat Lux (let there be light) of a second creation; because thence there came down upon the world the new law of a new civilization, the New Commandment as Christ Himself called it. On the day when it was said to the individual, 'Love God above all things and your neighbor as yourself for the love of God;'[3] to the citizen, 'Render to God the things that are God's and to Caesar the things that are Caesar's;'[4] to the State, 'Seek first the kingdom of God and its justice:'[5] on that day there arose a new morality, a new public law, a new social ideal. Like a mysterious leaven, the creative word worked upon and permeated humanity, and all the manifestations of justice and love there produced from century to century are but the result of this marvelous fermentation: 'The kingdom of heaven is like to leaven, which a woman took and hid in three measures of meal, until the whole was leavened.' "[6]

On the day when the Christian religion gave to mankind its compass and pointed out its polar star

[3] Mark XII. 30-31.
[4] Matthew XXII. 21.
[5] Matthew VI. 33.
[6] Matthew XIII. 33.

there began for humanity a life worth living, a life of which the ancient poet [7] seemed to have had an obscure presentiment when on the frontispiece of the new world he wrote this grand verse:

> Magnus ab integro saeculorum nascitur ordo.
> The great order of ages is born anew.

Then, walking under the shadow of the cross, the Christian centuries took the road of the future.[8]

> Vexilla Regis prodeunt.
> Crucis fulget mysterium.
> The royal banners now unfurled,
> The mystic cross illumines the world.

To perpetuate in the world this new civilization and keep its commands fresh in men's minds Christ organized a visible society of twelve men. For three years He taught them how to teach and spread His new civilization. No word was said, however, of the art of writing, printing or book-making. Sending them forth into every Nation He said: "All power is given to me in Heaven and in Earth—Going, therefore, teach ye all Nations." These teachers and their teaching are for everywhere, and are foreign only where God is foreign—"teaching them to observe all things whatsoever I have commanded you." This society is independent of civil rulers. "And behold,

---

[7] The ancient poet here quoted is Vergil.
[8] Opening lines of the Vespers hymn during the Passion-tide.

CATHOLIC DECLARATION OF SPIRITUAL INDEPENDENCE

"And I say unto you: That thou art Peter; and upon this rock I will build my church, and the gates of Hell shall not prevail against it."
Matt. XVI. 18.

DECLARATION OF AMERICAN INDEPENDENCE

"And for the support of this Declaration, with a firm reliance of the protection of Divine Providence, we mutually pledge to each other our lives, our fortunes, and our sacred honor."
Thomas Jefferson.

I am with you all days even to the consummation of the world." [9] It is independent of clime and time, and like God it is indestructible.

A chief executive was chosen for the new organization. To Simon, son of John, Christ said: "Thou art Peter (a Rock), and upon this rock I will build My Church, and the gates of Hell shall not prevail against it. And I will give to thee the Keys of the Kingdom of heaven. And whatsoever thou shalt bind upon earth, it shall be bound also in heaven: and whatsoever thou shalt loose on earth it shall be loosed also in heaven." [10]

Like leaven in the bosom of society these principles and commands operated to produce in time the blessings of justice, equality, truth, liberty and democracy. In a word, they created Christian Civilization.

Behold on opposite page the picture of the signing of the Declaration of Independence, the birth of our American Government in 1776. Politically the new world had reached a crisis similar to that of the old world on the eve of Christ's Birth. It needed a savior.

The Apostles of the New Nation are gathered with the first President in an historic room in Philadelphia. They are giving their hands and hearts to the political creed of the Republic. These men did

[9] Matthew XXVIII. 19, 20.
[10] Matthew XVI. 18, 19.

not meet to create some new political dogma,[11] but re-dedicated to humanity what was from the beginning revealed: namely, that God gave men life and liberty to pursue and overtake happiness. But why was it necessary to restate and redefine these truths? Because they were dimmed, obscured and abused by selfish and tyrannical kings who, by the superstition "that the King can do no wrong," stifled Christian democracy.

At the opening of the 150th anniversary of the Declaration of Independence, President Coolidge read this creed of American Independence, and stopping at the end of each idea said: "This truth is final." Yes, like the multiplication table, the Apostles' Creed and the Ten Commandments, the truths of the Declaration are final. They cannot be remade or reformed. They are eternal expressions of order and right fixed, and incapable of change for all time. To protest perpetually unto all men those God-given

---

[11] Words, like cards, have different values. In discussion, we must agree on the value and meaning of words, as in a card game players must agree on the value of the cards.

Now "Dogma" has been described by Protestants as "a screen which Catholics draw between the eyes of men and the Light of the Gospel." But Dogma means truth. Here are a few examples of Dogmas:

A dogma in Mathematics is $2 + 2 = 4$.
In History: President Coolidge in 1927.
In Astronomy: The sun is center of the solar system.
In Politics: No taxation without representation.
In Geography: Texas is the largest State in the Union.
In Logic: A thing cannot be black and white at the same time.
In Domestic Science: Too many cooks spoil the broth.
In Travel: "Danger; go slow."
In Religion: Christ is God.

blessings, man's natural right to life, liberty and justice—for which the Americans of 1776 bled, the Government of the United States was instituted.

We have placed the principles of the Declaration of American Independence and those of the Church side by side. Do you see any cause for conflict? Every principle of liberty and justice in the Declaration of Independence is contained in the greater Declaration of Christ, as a small circle is contained within a greater one. These principles of Church and State are but carbon copies of the one original in the Divine mind. The foundations of the Church and of the American State were laid by Him who laid the foundations of the World. For there are not two Gods and two sources of principle, but one God in Whom there is no contradiction.

The principles of the American Declaration, therefore, are Catholic. They have been taught by Catholic theologians in the 4th, 13th, 17th, 18th and 20th centuries.

THOMAS AQUINAS 13th Century	CARDINAL BELLARMINE 17th Century	THOMAS JEFFERSON 18th Century
The Sovereign has no power to frame laws except as representing the people.	*Secular* or *Civil Power* is instituted by men; it is in the people unless they bestow it on the prince. This power is immediately in the whole multitude as in the subject of it; for this power is in the divine law but	We hold these truths to be self-evident, that all men are created equal, that they are endowed by their Creator with certain inalienable Rights, that among these are Life, Liberty and the pursuit of Happiness.
A law is a rule of reason whose object is the common good, promulgated by him who has the care of society.		
In reality all power		

THOMAS AQUINAS
13th Century

proceeds from God but that it is not delegated to any particular individual directly unless by the will of Civil society. That this power is not vested directly in any individual but in the entire collection of men.

To secure to every one the possession of his rights God has constituted rulers to govern and rule.

When, however, laws are opposed to the common weal or have an improper aim they are injustices and not laws and when all lawful means to right the wrong have proven in vain, then forceful rebellion is justified provided the moral, intelligent and major part of the community are certain from the beginning of the tyranny and of the probable success of the rebellion.[12]

CARDINAL BELLARMINE
17th Century

the divine law hath given this power to no particular man.

If the positive law be taken away there is no reason why among a multitude who are equal one rather than another should bear rule over the rest.

Power is given by the multitude to one man or more, by the same law of nature, for the Commonwealth cannot exercise this power, therefore it is bound to bestow it upon some one man or some few. It depends on the will of the multitude to ordain over themselves a King, consul or other magistrates.

And if there be just cause the multitude may change the Kingdom into an aristocracy or democracy.[13]

THOMAS JEFFERSON
18th Century

That to secure these rights, Governments are instituted among men, deriving their just powers from the consent of the governed. That whenever any Form of Government becomes destructive of these ends, it is the Right of the People to alter or to abolish it, and to institute new Government, laying its foundation on such principles and organizing its powers in such form, as to them shall seem most likely to effect their Safety and Happiness.[14]

[12] St. Thomas Aquinas. 2-2-42-2 Ad. 3.
[13] Filmer's Compendium of Bellarmine's Philosophy.
[14] Declaration of Independence.

The Declaration of American Independence in its vital principles is but one page from the Book of Catholic doctrine. This fact you may get around, but you cannot get over it. Why raise the cry that the fundamental institutions of the Church are in conflict with those of the United States? There is a reason. These alarmists, in order to divert suspicion from themselves, seek, by the foulest means, to lay at the door of the Church and the Pope the crime of their own divided allegiance.

Let us see the facts. One article of American belief is the Separation of Church and State: "Each in its kind is supreme, each has fixed limits within which it is contained, limits which are defined by the nature and special object of the province of each." [15] Is this the traditional Protestant teaching and practice? From the beginning Protestantism united the spiritual and temporal, the Church and State, under one head and one crown: The King's. The King ruled by Divine right. He was absolute. He could do no wrong. Now read what a well-known Catholic theologian teaches on this point: "All power is from God but that it is not delegated to any particular individual directly, unless by the consent of civil society. We therefore consider erroneous the doctrine that God confers this power immediately and directly upon the King or any other head

---

[15] Pope Leo XIII: "Christian Constitution of States."

of supreme government to the exclusion of the express consent of the Public." [16]

In his excellent book, AMERICAN DEMOCRACY AND CATHOLIC DOCTRINE, Sylvester J. McNamara, M.A., says:

"The immediate effects of the Reformation in Scotland, according to the Protestant historians, McCrie, Mackintosh, Strickland and even Knox himself, were civil war, the destruction and confiscation of private property, and the denial of liberty of conscience—in a word, the fundamentals of democracy were destroyed.

"Does democracy owe anything to the Reformation? Nothing save its practical annihilation. In our rapid summary glance of its effects in the countries of England, Scotland, Germany, and Switzerland, we have seen it destroy the right to life, property and liberty: freedom of conscience, freedom of speech and freedom of the press. It was the cause of the decay of education and destruction of public charity. It added nothing new to the sum of existing democratic thought, but, on the contrary, popularized dogmas productive of absolute and arbitrary government in teaching the union of Church and State and the divine right of kings —two of the most pernicious doctrines ever conceived in the mind of men to destroy the political freedom of a people. Its dogma of private interpretation has been the actuating principle and justification of every religious fanatic and political anarchist who saw in himself an inspired prophet of God or the savior of a people from political bondage. History records no greater political servility than that fos-

[16] Concina: "Dogmatic and Moral Theology."

tered and established by the so-called Protestant Reformation.

"For it was not until the descendants of the reformers
divorced themselves from the doctrines of their founders
and wedded themselves to ancient Catholic political principles that they were able to give birth to modern democracy
as we know it."

Religious liberty is an article of American Faith.
"Congress shall make no law respecting an establishment of religion or prohibiting the free exercise
thereof." [17] "It cannot be denied," continues Mr.
McNamara, "that in England for over a century
after the beginning of the Reformation, religious
liberty—'the right to worship God according to the
dictates of one's conscience without thereby incur-
ring any civil penalties or disabilities'—was un-
known. Civil liberty depended upon religious con-
victions. The hundreds of lives forfeited for failure
to acknowledge the absolute spiritual and temporal
supremacy of the crown during the reigns of Henry,
Edward, Mary and Elizabeth, and the confiscation
of the material possessions of those who would not
assert the papacy of the sovereign, witness the denial
of the right to life, liberty and property."

With what sacredness the right of property was
held may be judged by an extract from BEFORE
THE GREAT PILLAGE, by Dr. Augustus Jessop,
an Honorary Fellow of Oxford and Cambridge Uni-

[17] Article I. Bill of Rights, Constitution of the United States."

versities and a minister of the Church of England. For over a quarter of a century Dr. Jessop made a minute examination of the original records still existing of English parish life in pre-Reformation times, and by patient and laborious work in this field of research, qualified himself as an authority. He writes:

"When I talk about the GREAT PILLAGE, I mean that horrible and outrageous looting of our churches other than conventual, and the robbing of the people of this country of property in land and movable, which property had actually been inherited by them as members of those organized religious communities known as parishes. It is necessary to emphasize the fact that in the general scramble of The Terror under Henry the Eighth and of the Anarchy in the days of Edward the Sixth, there was only one class that was permitted to retain any large portion of its endowments. The monasteries were plundered to their very pots and pans. Almshouses in which old men and women were fed and clothed were robbed to the last pound, the poor almsfolk being turned out into the cold at an hour's warning to beg their bread. Hospitals for the sick and needy, whose very raison d'être was that they were to look after and care for those who were past caring for themselves, these were stripped of all their belongings, the inmates sent out to hobble into some convenient dry ditch to lie down and die in, or to crawl into some barn or hovel, there to be tended, not without fear of consequence, by some kindly man or woman who could not bear to see a suffering fellow-creature drop down and die at their own door-posts.

"We talk with a great deal of indignation of the Tam-

many ring. The day will come when some one will write
the story of two other rings—the ring of miscreants who
robbed the monasteries in the reign of Henry the Eighth
was the first; but the ring of robbers who robbed the poor
and helpless in the reign of Edward the Sixth was ten
times worse than the first."

"The Universities only just escaped the general confiscation; the friendly societies and benefit clubs and guilds did
not escape. The accumulated wealth of centuries, their
houses and lands, their money, their vessels of silver and
their vessels of gold, their ancient cups and goblets and
salvers, even to their very chairs and tables, were set down
in inventories and catalogues, and all swept into the robbers' hoard. Last, but not least, the immense treasures in
the churches, the joy and boast of every man and woman
and child in England, who day by day and week by week
assembled to worship in the old houses of God, which they
and their fathers had built, and whose every vestment and
chalice, candlestick and banner, organs and bells, the picture and image, the altar and shrine, they looked upon as
their own and part of their birthright—all these were torn
away by the rudest spoilers, carted off, they knew not
whither, with jeers and scoffs and ribald shoutings, while
none dared to raise a hand or let his voice be heard above
the whisper of a prayer of bitter grief and agony." [18]

When the evil days came upon them and they were
forced to fly to America, many of those religious
revolutionists felt the value of the things they had
thrown away, and returned to Catholic political

---

[18] Quoted by Sylvester J. McNamara, M.A.: "American Democracy and Catholic Doctrine," p. 61.

principles. But the history of the Colonies of the United States shows that many others brought with them the hates and fears and beliefs which caused the Great Pillage in the Old Land. Since 1776 history points to hundreds of institutions, daughters of Old World Protestantism, that are foreign to the genius and traditions of America. As a consequence there are encamped on our soil scores of institutions whose principles are in open conflict with the traditions of the United States. This is base ingratitude. It is biting the hand that feeds.

Those who raise the cry that Catholics are unfit to hold public office in the United States, hope amid the tumult and the shouting to divert attention from themselves by accusing the Pope and the Church. But no one is deceived. It is history repeating itself. When Nero burnt Rome he accused the Christians in order to take the eyes of mankind from himself.

III

SUPREME COURT OF THE CHURCH

"He that heareth you heareth me."   (Luke X. 16.)

WHEN God in the person of Christ had organized the Church, He set up His Supreme Court, not to add or subtract or to create new beliefs, but to be forever a living witness to the teachings and traditions once delivered by Him to His Apostles. "Teaching them to observe all things whatsoever I have commanded you, and behold I am with you all days even to the consummation of the world." [1] This Court is supreme in the spiritual domain in all things whatsoever Christ commanded. It is concerned with the Word of God only. "Hold the traditions which you have learned, whether by word, or by our epistle." [2]

This Supreme Court of the Church gives short, clear, explicit definitions of truth already revealed by Christ—God, and His apostles, to be held by all His followers. These definitions of revealed truth are forever unassailable, that is to say, infallible. They are the expression or carbon copy of the Di-

[1] Matthew XXVIII. 19-20.
[2] II. Thess. II. 14.

23

vine Will, Which first enunciated them. Christ did not explain all things to His apostles, but said to the Church: "Going therefore teach," that is define, explain and apply to every varied necessity and condition, in every age and clime "all things whatsoever I have commanded you." [3]

"He that heareth you heareth me." [4] Time will tell. "Heaven and earth shall pass away, but my words will not pass away." [5] The institution of a Supreme teaching authority is absolutely necessary in view of man's nature and for the public good. It is necessary in the Church, and it is necessary in the State. It is one of those things we hold as self-evident truths. For reason demands a final tribunal of an infallible authority to deal with manifest corruptions of doctrine.

The power of this Supreme infallible authority operates to protect the individual against his own weakness, and the multitude against partial judgments of individuals. Christ knew what was in man. He knew that original sin had darkened man's understanding, weakened his will and made him selfish. Each man's private teaching, explanation, application and interpretation of law would naturally be influenced by selfishness, ignorance, pride and passion. It would breed division, dissension, chaos and contradiction in any society anywhere. In ninety-

[3] Mark XXVIII. 19-20.
[4] Luke X. 16.
[5] Luke XXI. 33.

nine cases out of one hundred justice would be frustrated.

Now a principle of action is true in the civil and political order only when it is true in the ethical or moral order. Therefore, whenever the private interpretation and application of the law is wrong in the moral order, it is wrong and immoral in the civil and political order. It becomes a disruptive principle.

The Declaration of Independence is one of the corner-stones of our government. It is a stone hewn from the Rock on which the Church is built. But how shall each individual citizen know absolutely if his political life is in harmony with the principles of the Declaration and the Constitution? There are two ways: That God, the author of these principles, walk again among men and direct their lives accordingly, or that He delegate angels or men with authority to unfold to each one in every particular circumstance and controversy, the meaning and application of the laws.

This last is exactly what He did. God deals with men by and through men. All authority is from God. But since God did not place political authority directly in one particular man—for all men are equal —it is placed in the entire population, which transfers it to one or several who hold and rule in the name of and for the benefit of all.

At once the Fathers of the new American nation in

the first Session of Congress during 1789, set up the Supreme Court headed by a Supreme Justice. This Court is the living, continuous witness to the teachings and traditions written into the Declaration and Constitution and handed down from generation unto generation. The Supreme Court is a moral power out of the reach of selfish material aims. In 1788 Jefferson wrote to Madison: "Wherever there is an interest or power to do wrong, wrong will generally be done."

Our United States Supreme Court—a moral person—is more than one hundred and fifty years old and yet young. It is young with the youth of Washington and Jefferson and Lincoln. It is strong with the strength of God's authority. It does not create new political dogmas or creeds or add to or subtract from the principles of the Declaration. Its duty is to give clear, explicit declarations, manifestations and applications of particular principles of justice and right once delivered by the Fathers, as self-evident truths, and set in the organic law of the land. The Declaration and Constitution receive no new addition whenever one of its principles is explained or applied to a particular case. The decision is not a new law but the application of an existing one. The principles are final, but their application may vary with clime and time.

The declarations and definitions of the Supreme Court must be accepted as final by all citizens within the shores of America. They are unassailable in this sense, that there is on earth for the American citizen no higher Civil Court to which he may appeal. He is a political heretic who would by word or act set his individual self against the decisions of that Supreme Teaching Body. Such acts give aid and comfort to the enemies of our country and its people. And he may be punished not by excommunication [6] only but by jail or death.

In setting up, or rather in laying down, the foundation of the American Government—the greatest piece of work ever devised by man—the builders had before them these two plans: The Protestant invention of private interpretation by the individual with all his private virtues and vices, emotions, sentiments, passions and prejudices influencing, shaping and coloring his final judgments; and on the other hand, there was the Catholic institution of a Supreme teaching body lawfully constituted to render final judgments through a Supreme Justice.

The American patriots of 1776 applied the Catholic plan in establishing their Courts, to interpret, teach, explain and apply the laws and be final in their judgments. The plan of the Protestants— namely, the liberty of the subject and the citizen to conclude what he pleased from the law and be to himself—right or wrong——the last Court of Appeal, would work out only in a country where there was merely one man, as on the island of Tobago

---

[6] "Civil excommunication" implies physical punishment. "Church excommunication" implies loss of the right to the Sacraments.

where Robinson Crusoe was monarch of all he surveyed—from center all around to the sea—lord of the fowl and the brute.

If the Protestant principles of private interpretation and union of Church and State had been applied to the American Nation, we would not now have one nation indivisible with liberty and justice for all, but more than 120 million opinions and side-shows, and only the tattered and torn fragments of a nation. In fine, a condition of political life like unto the babel of confusion now present in the religious non-Catholic world, offspring of that world which revolted against the immemorial authority of Christendom in the sixteenth century.

IV

THE BIBLE AND THE CONSTITUTION

"Go forward, in one hand bearing the Book of Christian Truth
and in the other the Constitution of the United States!"
                                        Cardinal Satolli.

FROM whom did the Church get Her Constitution?
Let me answer this other question first, Where did
we get the Constitution of the United States? Some
eleven years after the government had established
its Supreme Judicial Department, we got the Constitution of the United States.

The Constitution of the United States is that fundamental law which makes secure the people's rights,
and which directs and governs those who exercise
the powers of the National Government. It gives
Legislative, Executive and Judicial powers to the
government to make laws, execute and interpret
them. Besides the written document of the Constitution there are certain unwritten laws which, by
custom, experience and tradition, have the force
of law among the people. In its framework the
Constitution of the United States is modeled on
that of the Constitution of the Dominican and Jesuit

Orders, ancient religious regiments within the ancient Church.

Now where did we get the Constitution of the Church? From Christ, and in the Bible which we received from the Church, we have the historical record of that Constitution. The Bible is a collection of seventy-two books written between the years 1500 B. C. and 100 A. D. These were bound into one volume during the fourth century by the Pope and Bishops of the Church.

Now for the creation of the New Testament of the Bible, what provision did Christ make through His Prophets, by His own words and example? First, He did not predict its creation. He Himself never left a line of writing nor a word. His only writing was written in the dry sand where the record of many faults should be written. He never while on earth hinted anywhere during His three years of teaching that the Apostles should write. Christ never saw the entire Bible. The Doctors marveled, however, at His knowledge of the Old Law. Not one of His Apostles saw the entire Bible or even the entire New Testament. But Christ did say: "Going therefore teach ye all nations: Teaching them to observe all things whatsoever I have commanded you." [1] Now it is natural to ask how were these mere men, the Apostles, to remember all things Christ commanded they should teach all Nations and every creature until the end of the world. Christ

[1] Matthew XXVIII. 19-20.

answered: "These things have I spoken to you, abiding with you. But the Paraclete, the Holy Ghost, whom the Father will send in My Name, He will teach you all things, and bring all things to your mind, whatsoever I shall have said to you." [2]

But all things whatsoever Christ commanded His Apostles to teach are not contained in the Bible. At least the Bible says so: "But there are also many other things which Jesus did: which if they were written every one, the world itself, I think, would not be able to contain the books that should be written." [3] The Bible consequently is not a complete guide to all things whatsoever Christ commanded. The Church is. "I am with you all days, even to the consummation of the world." "He that heareth you heareth me." How then came into the world the oldest Book of Books? In this manner: About seventy years after the Church was organized to teach all Nations, St. John finished his Gospel or diary of the Life of Christ.

At the Councils of Hippo 393 A. D., Rome 394, Carthage 397, the Supreme Court, the Pope and Bishops collected the Gospels and diaries written by the Apostles and Disciples of Christ, and put them into one book and called it the New Testament. To this collection they added the fifty-five books of the Old Law which they received from the Synagogues. The Supreme Court at the Council of Trent in

[2] John XIV. 25-26.
[3] John XXI. 25.

1545-1563, and at the Council of the Vatican in 1870 confirmed the decisions which the Councils of Hippo, Rome and Carthage concluded about the Bible in the fourth century.

Is the Bible then a complete witness of the Church from the beginning? The Bible was not published till the end of the fourth century. It was therefore but a partial witness to the first great victories of the Church over the pagan and barbarous world. The foundations of Christian civilization were laid by the Church before the Bible was published. Besides this, the Bible is not a living witness at all, because it has no life at all, and does not belong to the category of living things. The Bible is deaf, dumb and blind. We need to make it live and hear testimony, a living voice, the voice of a supreme authority.

During the most fruitful years of the Church's life, the first three centuries, the Bible was so rare that few people could have seen it; and when in the fourth century it was published—indeed, as late as the fifteenth century, when printing was invented —not one in 100,000 people could have a Bible. Protestants have generally fallen into the error of connecting the scarcity of Bibles with the Catholic Church. The Church is not responsible for the lack of human inventive genius which, until the fifteenth century, failed to invent printing. Bibles were rare and costly because makers of books were rare. It took an artist some ten years to copy out the whole

Bible. He must have received at least three dollars a day, which placed the cost of one copy of the Bible at $8,000.

Now if Christianity evangelized the known world for fifteen hundred years without a Bible, the Bible was not absolutely necessary to its existence, growth and progress. If God had intended that the Bible should be a condition to the existence of the Church, He would have found a means from the beginning of placing that condition within the reach of all.

Today, in the twentieth century, only fifty per cent. of the earth's inhabitants can read the Bible, and of that number not twenty per cent. have read the entire Bible of Seventy-Two Books, and not five per cent. of the very learned understand the meaning of all and every part of it. Not a single individual in the world today can say that the Bible —the English translation—is a true copy of the originals for the very reason that the originals do not exist. The oldest copy of the Old Law (in Hebrew) we possess, was made in the tenth century, and the oldest manuscript of the New Testament (in Greek,) was made in the fourth century, and these are not the original copies. Since we cannot summon at will, from the dead, the writers of the first copies to tell us if we have a true translation, how shall we be certain we have a Bible at all?

Because the infallible teaching of the Church tells us that the Bible is the Word of God, we believe it to be so. The Church has taken such care of the Sacred Bible that we find in the Vatican Library today parts of Gospels "written with silver ink on purple parchment with the Divine names in gold." [4] The Catholic Church edited the Bible; she translated it; she nursed it. From fire and danger, from pillage and persecution, from haters of God and man she guarded it. With the invention of printing she gave it to the world.

Now where does the open conflict exist between these two institutions—the Constitution of the Church and the Constitution of the State? Both Constitutions are but copies of the original principles of Law and Order in the Divine Mind within which there is no conflict. The rule of political faith for the American citizen is not the Constitution only, but the Constitution as unfolded, applied, interpreted and explained to us by the Supreme Court of the United States. The rule of religious faith for the Catholic is the revealed word of God explained, interpreted and unfolded to us by the Supreme Tribunal of the Church.

For unity of belief there must be unity of interpretation. When one Doctor's interpretation contradicts another's, who will settle the question? Both cannot be right at the same time. Naturally God could walk again among us and settle it, but since His Ascension into Heaven He speaks through His

[4] Msgr. E. Tisserant, Assistant to the Librarian of the Vatican Library.

agents, mostly men. He answers all questions of controversy by pointing to Peter and Peter's successors to whom he says: "Going therefore teach," explain and define and interpret, "to all nations and to every creature, all things I have commanded you: and behold I am with you all days, even to the consummation of the world." [5] "He that heareth you heareth me." [6]

In the United States we answer all questions of controversy by pointing to the Supreme Court, whose decisions are final and unassailable. Here we have made another discovery, a third striking kinship and parallel between the Constitutional principles and methods of the Republic and those of the Church.

[5] Matthew XXVIII. 19-20.
[6] Luke X. 16.

V

RELIGIOUS AND POLITICAL HERESIES

"That they all may be one, as Thou, Father, in me, and I in Thee; that they also may be one in us; that the world may believe that Thou hast sent me."

St. John XVII. 21.

"Mutantur homines per sacra, non mutantur sacra per homines!"

"Men should be changed by religion, not religion by men!"
(General of Augustinians at the Council of Trent.)

"We cannot produce the Christianity of Jesus Christ by union of all the differences which were not founded upon His teachings. We would still have only a compromise."
Harold Bell Wright ("God and the Groceryman").

HOW DOES THE CHURCH TREAT HER RELIGIOUS HERESIES?

THE Church has had and always will have to combat heresy. Heresy means division. St. Peter speaks of false teachers among Christians, who will bring in heresies of perdition.[1] Heresy is error contrary to revealed truth and tenaciously adhered to by one who professes to be a Christian. A heretic is one who refuses to believe one or more of the Articles of Faith determined by the Supreme authority of

[1] II. Peter II. 1.

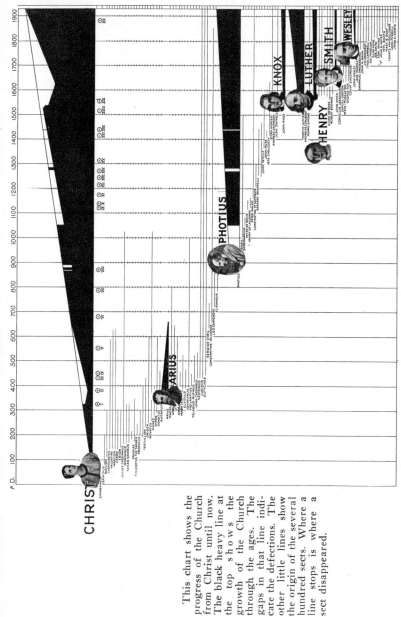

This chart shows the progress of the Church from Christ until now. The black heavy line at the top shows the growth of the Church through the ages. The gaps in that line indicate the defections. The other little lines show the origin of the several hundred sects. Where a line stops is where a sect disappeared.

The above chart is reproduced by the courtesy of THE VINCENTIAN PRESS.

the Universal Church to whom Christ said: "I am with you all days, even to the consummation of the world." [2] "He that heareth you, heareth me." [3]

Formal heresy is rebellion against God Who requires us to submit to the teachings of His Church. In the course of nineteen hundred years many heresies have sprung up in the path of the Church. In the picture set forth you will observe some of the principal heresies, the time and place of their rise, their fall, decay or final disappearance.

THE ARIAN HERESY, for example, sprang up in the early part of the fourth century and ceased to exist in the seventh. Arius denied the Divinity of Christ. This error was condemned by the Supreme Court of the Church at the First Council of Nicæa in 325 A. D., and the true doctrine already contained in revelation was explained and defined, namely: that Christ is true God and true man.

THE NESTORIAN HERESY took its rise in the first part of the fifth century. Nestorius maintained that there are two distinct persons in Christ, one Divine and the other human, and he claimed that Mary was the Mother of the human person only. He was condemned by the Supreme Court of the Church at the Council of Ephesus 431, which on this occasion added to the liturgy of the Church, the prayer: Holy Mother of God.

[2] Matthew XXVIII. 20.
[3] Luke X. 16.

THE GREEK SCHISM arose during the second half of the ninth century. Up to that time there was no Greek orthodox Catholic Church. In the middle of the ninth century the Greek Emperor deposed Patriarch Ignatius of Constantinople, and in his place appointed a layman, whose name was Photius. The Supreme Court of the Church under Pope Nicholas set aside the layman and restored the rightful Patriarch, and unity was once more established in the Church. But in the middle of the eleventh century the great separation came. The principal reason now was the jealousy of the Orient at the growing prestige of the Roman See. Near-unity was again established in the last half of the thirteenth and the first part of the fifteenth century. The Greek Church is the only non-Catholic body that could return in a body for the reason that the one thing required of them would be recognition of and submission to the Holy See.

PROTESTANTISM IN GERMANY originated in the beginning of the sixteenth century with Martin Luther, a priest of the Order of St. Augustine who left his Order and the Church. He rejected the Sacrifice of the Mass, the Supremacy of the Pope, and Five of the Seven Sacraments. He was a brilliant fanatic, but put his brains against the mind of God. Christianity is a religion of self-denial, for Christ had said: "If any man will come after me, let him deny himself, and take up his cross, and follow me." [4] Luther's religion was: "Faith without good works is sufficient for salvation." When Luther led his followers into rebellion against the immemorial authority of the Church, his followers led a rebellion against the authority of the State, which drew from Luther himself these words: "The world grows worse and worse, and becomes more wicked day by day." Lutheranism in America is divided into twenty-two sects.

PROTESTANTISM IN ENGLAND came into existence in the beginning of the sixteenth century, in the days of King Henry the Eighth. Henry was a devout Catholic king, showing his loyalty by denouncing Luther's revolt in a book which earned for him the title of "Defender of the Faith"—the Catholic Faith—which title the English crown still retains. But it was when Henry demanded a divorce from his lawful wife Catherine that the king's faith was tested. To such a request Pope Clement could but reply: "What therefore God hath joined together, let no man put asunder." [5] Blinded by passion, pride and power Henry declared himself Pope of the Church as well as head of the State. He plundered the cathedrals, monasteries and Church properties, and many of his followers to this day live on the fat of sacrilege.

In the year 1534 Henry caused Parliament to issue

[4] Matthew XVI. 24.
[5] Mark X. 9.

an act for the submission of the will of the Clergy to the will of the King: "If any man teach any matter contrary to the instructions of the King, he shall suffer the penalty of death by burning with the forfeiture to the King of all his goods and chattels." [6]

It was determined by the King that all Catholics must be disloyal, and when they proved 200% loyal it made matters worse. It was further determined that the word Catholic was a term of reproach and straight away it became so. England never did give up the faith. It was stolen from her. Nor was it an easy matter to rob a people of the faith which they had professed for ten centuries. Lord Macaulay, the great Protestant leader, thus described the character of the persons who did the job:

"A king whose character may be best described by saying that he was despotism itself personified; unprincipled ministers, a rapacious aristocracy, a servile parliament, such were the instruments by which England was delivered from the yoke of Rome. The work which had been begun by Henry the murderer of his wives, was continued by Somerset the murderer of his brother, and completed by Elizabeth the murderer of her guest. Of those who had any important share in bringing the 'reformation' about, Ridley was perhaps the only person who did not consider it as a mere political job."

But a new movement seems at hand for certain elements of the Episcopal Church. We have read in the Press that certain prominent members of that

[6] Statutes of Realm III. 896.

branch of the Protestant Church are crying out, pleading for unity with the Mother Church. The Laużanne Conference on "Faith and Order" in 1927 met with unity as its watchword. Now the English State Church has declared by the revision of its Prayer book, that what was believed to be true at the Reformation is now false; that all who believed in those teachings were for all these 400 years in error. This is a sorry and a salutary admission! Some want to return to their father's house— The Catholic Church—others will go into the unnumbered ranks of agnosticism, infidelity and naturalism. In the words of Lincoln: "For 400 years they tried to secede from the universal union of the universal Church, but their secession was not a success."

THE PRESBYTERIAN GROUP differs from other protestant sects in this that the Calvinistic doctrine of Predestination receives special emphasis; and each sect is governed by representative bodies of Elders. Its previous claims to historic continuity from the Apostles have been refuted by Presbyterian scholars. Calvin founded Presbyterianism in Switzerland and John Knox, a renegade Scotch priest, became his disciple. It was Knox who carried Calvin's teachings to Scotland. In 1560 a Confession of Faith was sanctioned by the Scotch Parliament. The Apostle of Presbyterianism in America is Rev. Francis Makennie of Ireland. Today Presbyterianism is split into seventeen varieties.

THE BAPTIST CHURCH was organized in England in the first quarter of the seventeenth century by Mr. John Smyth. This gentleman claimed that the true Church became extinct, and that it was his duty to found it anew. To this end he baptized himself and thirty-six others, and the Church was constituted. To escape the protestant persecution of England, Mr. Roger Williams, a minister of the English Church by law established, fled to America in 1631. He came into conflict with the government, however, and was banished from the Massachusetts Colony. He found a refuge in Rhode Island where he founded the Baptist Church in the year 1639. The Baptists are divided into seventeen denominations with other divisions on the way.

THE METHODIST CHURCH traces its history to Oxford, England, where John and Charles Wesley organized a little band of students of religious disposition and called their union "the Methodists." When the union disbanded, John and Charles sailed to America and landed at Savannah, Georgia, in the year 1735, about 200 years after Columbus had planted the Cross on the soil of America. In Georgia John became associated with the Rev. Mr. Spangenber, a Moravian Bishop. According to histories of the Colony and State of Georgia, written by Bishop Stevens and Charles Johnson, Jr., when young Wesley came to the Colony of Georgia under Oglethorpe's administration he was still a loyal English Churchman. Testimonies of witnesses before grand jury proceedings in Case of Causton vs. Wesley show Wesley to have begun the preaching of a strange doctrine during his missionary work (about 1736) among the settlers and Indians. His own biography states Wednesday evening, May 1, 1739 in London, England as being the date of the beginning of the Methodist Society. Methodism in the United States began in 1766 with a local preacher, Philip Embury. At the request of Mrs. Barbara Hicks he preached a sermon in his own house. This beginning increased and multiplied and today there are in the United States some twenty-two varieties bearing the same name—and the end is not yet.

CHRISTIAN SCIENCE owes its existence to Mrs. Mary Baker Glover Patterson Eddy, who as a young girl heard strange voices in the air. Her father said of her: "If Mary Magdalen had seven devils, my Mary has ten." As she grew she cultivated a taste for philosophy. She married a gentleman called Patterson and divorced him. Her second husband's name was Mr. Eddy. He met his death by "Mesmeric Poison mentally administered," said the postmortem examination. In the year 1878 she "Invented" a philosophy and housed it in a Church.

This system denies the Blessed Trinity and the Divinity of Christ. What it does not recognize is that miraculous healing by prayer has been taught in the Catholic Church for twenty centuries. Christian Scientists have taken one truth or dogma of the Church and tried to magnify it into a complete religion and system of worship. In good faith they may secure the blessings of God in return for prayer, but they have sacrificed the whole for a mere crumb of the true faith.

HOW DOES THE UNITED STATES TREAT HER POLITICAL HERESIES?

Let us now examine a few samples of "political" heresies from the history of the United States. The United States is still young; only one hundred and fifty years have passed over her. Yet heresy has brought Uncle Sam's venerable head more than a dozen gray hairs. A political heresy may be described as an opinion contrary to the Declaration of Independence, the Constitution and decisions of the Supreme Court of the United States. It is a consequence of private interpretation. A political heresy promotes division, dissension and chaos. It gives comfort to the enemies of the country. It promotes rebellion.

In the printed chart of political heresies which we have placed parallel with the chart of the Church heresies you will observe, that right in the beginning of the republic we had to contend with Shay's Rebellion. A group of citizens sought to silence the voice of the Supreme Court, and institute mob rule in its stead. In consequence they were declared heretical and their leaders condemned.

THE NULLIFICATION ACT of J. C. Calhoun in 1833 was an attempt on the part of one political group to set aside a law of Congress. The great Daniel Webster, however, pointed out that only the Supreme Court possessed such powers.

THE CIVIL WAR was but the offspring of private interpretation and application of the law. The sad spectacle of a divided nation, two Presidents and an appeal to arms was the inevitable result.

THE A. P. A. HERESY of 1891 lasted six years. This secret society bound its members by oath "at all times to endeavor to place the political positions of this government in the hands of Protestants to the entire exclusion of Roman Catholics." The founder and the organizer of this heretical sect in the United States was one Mr. Henry Bowers. Its leaders grew fat over night on calumnies and forgeries. It was condemned in the severest terms by Theodore Roosevelt, and resolutions condemned and excommunicated by means of resolutions at the Democratic and Republican conventions.

THE COMMUNISTIC MOVEMENT tried to gain a foothold in the United States during 1914. In striking at private property, and the duty of government to protect unto every man what is his, the communists struck a blow at the basis of patriotism. When a citizen by his industry accumulates property, it becomes, so to speak, part of himself, and therefore he is always ready to fight in its defense, and if necessary lay down his life to protect his fireside. "If there is no personal God there are no masters of wealth" says the Communist, and therefore no man has an inalienable right to call this or that his and not another's. This principle they carried into society, advocating the doctrine of free love. A recent article on "Results of Communism in Russia" mentions four million children abandoned by their parents, who have launched themselves into the new pleasures and privileges of free love. One of their leaders, Eugene Debs, was apprehended at the instance of President Wilson and found guilty by a Federal Jury of attempting to incite to disloyalty, to incite, provoke and encourage resistance in the United States, and to promote the cause of the enemy. The lower Court sentenced him to ten years in the penitentiary; and on March 10, 1919 the United States Supreme Court sustained the conviction and sentence. He was finally pardoned through Executive Clemency.

THE HERESY OF THE KU KLUX KLAN SPRANG UP IN 1918, seized the government by the throat and, in the name of the Imperial Wizard, bade her fall down and adore. A private citizen, one Mr. Hiram Evans, elected himself Super-President of the United States and voted himself a super-salary. It is said that there were six million super-citizens who gave first allegiance to the Grand Dragon and his fiery cross, and second preference to the President of the United States and the American Flag.

The Klan's Declaration of Independence was: "It is a self-evident fact that only native born Protestant Americans hath God created free and equal." Its Constitution: "Only white native bred American Protestants are fit for civilization or eligible to an office or public trust under these Ku Klux States." For the leaders, the Klan became a get-rich-quick scheme. They grew wealthy and fat on the spoils of hate, violence, bigotry and murder. They specialized in "waylaying defenceless men and women and subjecting them to brutal assault." The Supreme Court of the United States finally excommunicated the Usurping Klan with all its works and pomp in the Oregon Test case. The Klan is dead but not sufficiently rotten for another of the species to spring up from its remains.

The third department of our government, the executive power, we have placed side by side with the same department in the Church. Is there in the executive department of the Church any cause for conflict with the State? We confess that we see none. The State follows the procedure of the Church in correcting, as one having authority, doctrines in con-

flict with the Constitution and the decisions of
the Supreme Court. Americanism is not an opinion.
It purges national institutions of men who
embody principles and standards alien to the traditions of the Republic and the policies of the
State.

The State is a visible human society with power to
punish, here and now, heretical and rebellious citizens by fines, imprisonments and death. She maintains her jails, electric chairs, and gallows. The
Church, a Divine visible society, withholds from the
heretic or the renegade her sacraments only, and
leaves the temporal punishment to those thorns of
remorse which lodge in his bosom to sting him. She
prays for all sinners in the daily Sacrifice of the Altar, and leaves the final judgment to God, trusting
always in His mercy.

The Divine Founder commissioned His Church
not to depart from the deposit of primitive truth
by a hair's breadth. "Teaching them to observe all
things whatsoever I have commanded you." [7] The
Bishops of the world are ever on the watchtower to
sound the alarm whenever the sacred citadel of primitive truth is attacked. Then Rome speaks and the
case is finished. In like manner our United States
Supreme Court is intolerant of every basic truth
in the Declaration and the Constitution. Loyalty to
the Constitution is political liberty. Loyalty to the
Commandments is moral liberty. Loyalty to truth is

[7] Matthew XXVIII. 20.

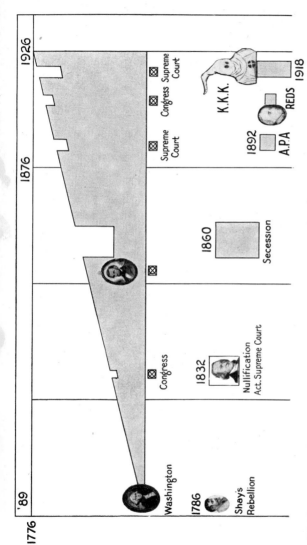

THIS CHART SHOWS THE TRIUMPH OF THE UNITED STATES

The shaded graph shows the growth of the United States from 3,000,000 to 120,000,000.
The gaps in the shaded graph are political schisms.
Right under are the decisions which condemned these schisms.
Below are pictures of the leaders of revolts.
Behold the strength and unity of the United States Government!
Behold the weakness and disunity of the political sects!

intellectual liberty. Only within the law and within the truth is man free.

Recently a Catholic editor challenged the Protestant leaders to show cause for their opposition to the ancient religion, with the result that the confessions of faith of the leading Protestant divisions and subdivisions were published in the Forum Magazine. Readers of the Forum now looked for facts hitherto concealed from the world by the Church. They looked for reason and logic and lo! we were treated to a potpourri of words—words—words— and besides that nothing. Putting all their tangled conceptions together, and taking their least common multiples we find that their gospel amounts to this: "We must have license to think, write, say and do as we please, and should any authority say nay, let him be anathema." Such an attitude in politics would amount to red radicalism and open treason against the civil government. Their air of infallibility in expressing private opinions is in striking contrast with that of the Holy Father, who calls himself the Servant of the Servants of God.

What they do not know is that the whims and criticisms of their congregations bear more heavily on those "apostles of absolute liberty" than did the authority of the Pope during any period of history. Twice in four centuries the Church made a pronouncement on the Word of God to be held by the entire Church. Outside the Word of God there lies a vast field of science and history, philosophy and theology, where giant intellects including the Pope, may wrestle with the greatest liberty and freedom of thought. What they do not know is that liberty is conformity to law—loyalty to the Law of God. That they are conscious of the evils of free thought on matters of religious principle; conscious of the distance they have drifted from Apostolic teaching without the guidance of Apostolic authority; conscious of the scandals to non-Christians of a Church broken up into hundreds and hundreds of shreds and patches with hundreds of others on the way is evident.

In the month of August, 1927, the leaders of the Protestant divisions and subdivisions met at Lauzanne in Switzerland. In the spirit of humble prayer they besought God to show them the way to unity and peace from heresy and schism. Let us applaud this effort of good will. This movement toward unity is the admission of the existence of schism. Well do they know the sad results of division, dissension, chaos and contradiction. The Catholic Church alone was absent from that meeting. Why? The Protestants were looking for unity of belief. The Catholic Church has it. The Protestants were seeking unity of government. The Catholic Church has it. The Protestants were looking among their various factions for the ONE, HOLY, CATHOLIC and APOSTOLIC Church which Christ founded on the Rock of Peter, the Church to which Christ spoke those words: "Behold I am with you all days even to the consummation of the world." [8] The Catholic Church claims to be that Church. No other Church claims it. The Catholic Church is the Church they were looking for at Lauzanne. They have eyes but see not.

Let us now glance at the position of the political heresies of the United States and ask: What man in his senses would claim that one brand of Americanism is as good as another; that the A. P. A. faction is equally as good as the Americanism of Washington, Lincoln and Coolidge? Who will maintain—and still retain his reason—that Mr. Hiram Evans, super-President of the K. K. K. variety of Americanism, holds political succession from Washington and Lincoln? With less show of reason it may be said that one brand of the Christian religion is as good as another: that Arius, Nestorius, Luther, Henry the Eighth, Calvin, Knox, John Wesley, Roger Williams, Mrs. Eddy or Mrs. Amie Semple McPherson broke into the line of Apostolic succession between St. Peter and Pius XI. As none of these men or women recall the portrait of Christ or his Apostles, so none of the founders of political anti-American factions recall the character likeness of Washington or Lincoln or Roosevelt. To none of these men or women did Christ say: "As the Father hath sent me I also send you." To no king or other head of civil government did Christ say: "Teach all nations." "He that heareth you heareth me." To

[8] Matthew XXVIII. 20.

none of these modern Christian sects did Christ say: "I am with you all days even to the consummation of the world." To none of these was victory promised forever: "The gates of hell shall not prevail against it."

Look once again at the government of the United States. During the first fifty years of the Republic, many political heresies were condemned by the United States government. The United States condemns them today, and will always condemn them.

In the first seven hundred years of Christianity twenty heresies were condemned by the Primitive Church. The Catholic Church condemns them today, because the Catholic Church is identical with the Primitive Church. The Protestant Churches have made these same heresies part and parcel of their belief. These primitive heresies were built on some compromise with Christ's teachings. The Protestant sects were built on these same compromises.

The only historic succession which the Protestant Churches may boast of is their historic kinship and relationship and succession from the heresies condemned by the Early Church. The heresies of the ages are their portion and their inheritance. The continuity of the condemnation bears witness to the continuity of the Primitive Church in the Catholic Church today.

Are the methods of the executive department of the United States in open conflict with the executive department of the Church? If the United States is

.represented by the principles of A. P. A.-ism, Communism, and K. K. K.-ism, the methods of the Church are in conflict with the United States. If the United States is represented by the Presidents, the Constitution and the Supreme Court, then the United States is in principle and practice a parallel of the Government of the Catholic Church.

VI

THE POPE

"The proudest royal house is but as yesterday compared with the line of Supreme Pontiffs." Lord Macaulay.

WE now draw a parallel between the line of Popes and Presidents, the office of the one and the other. If between the Papacy and the Presidency there is conflict, the Popes and the Presidents will tell us about it. Of course there will always be people, exceptions, who pretend to have more Catholicity than the Pope and more Americanism than the President. Such funny folks we have always with us.

Who and what is the Pope? The word Pope means father. His office is Bishop of Rome, Successor of St. Peter, and Head of the Catholic Church. Besides these he has other titles of preeminence and of honor.

The Church—a Divine visible organization—must have a visible head. In the Scriptures the Church is spoken of as a "body." [1] Without a head or with several heads, a human being is a hideous monstrosity. A Church or nation without a head or with several is no less hideous a spectacle. God himself appointed St. Peter head of the Church. The Church

[1] Ephes. IV. 3-6.

through the College of Cardinals throughout the world elects his successor. Any Catholic now living—regardless of race, color or nationality—may be elected Pope. Two hundred and sixty-one Popes have ruled the Church through the centuries. One hundred and four were Romans, one hundred and three were Italians, fifteen were French, nine Greeks, seven Germans, five Asiatics, three Africans, eight Spaniards, and two Dalmatians. England, Thrace, Holland, Portugal and Palestine gave one each.

The record of the Popes, their names, the time of their election, the years they reigned and the date of their deaths from St. Peter to Pius XI, is as complete and authentic as the historic succession of the Presidents of the United States from Washington to Coolidge. The Pope is head of the Church. He is Spiritual Father to more than 330,000,000 quite as if these all lived in one family, in one house. He is the Guardian of revealed truth. These two offices were created by Christ and were filled by Peter I and his successors for nineteen hundred years. A great Protestant scholar has recently said that the Pope as Supreme Father receives a loyalty that is the shame of Protestantism. Certain non-Catholic writers associate the Pope with despotism. Popery, they say, holds despotic sway over the human mind.

Now despotism is defined as power uncontrolled by man. In this sense every law of God in the physical and spiritual universe is a despotism—laws from which beautiful order and sublime harmony arise.

Dante expresses it thus:

"A law of order reigns
  Throughout Creation, and this law it is
  Which like to God the universe maintains,
  Herein do creatures see displayed
  The trace of the eternal might and this
  The end for which such ordinance was made.
  All natures to this heavenly law incline,
  Approaching each according to its kind
  Some more, some less unto their source Divine."

Take away these laws and all order and harmony
will disappear. In like manner the laws which com-
pel the use of food and drink and clothes and shel-
ter for our bodies are despotism. Do we try to lib-
erate ourselves from these things in order to achieve
greater freedom? Are the laws which regulate our
Spiritual Life less worthy of obedience than those
which regulate our physical being?

Take the man who has reached his seventieth
birthday. What independent moments has he experienced? For twenty-three years he was slave to the
infallible authority of sleep. The imperative call of
food and drink deprived him of his liberty to get
away from hunger—and that to the extent of three
and one-half years. Nor is he independent of the
law of the bath tub, the barber shop and talcum
powder, clothes and raiment to cover his nakedness.
These inanimate objects command as one having
authority and exact obedience to the tune of four

or five years. For fifteen years he is dependent on and subject to the authority of a teacher while he learns to walk and talk, read, write and count. Twenty-five years, at least, are sacrificed to the law of work, to earn by the sweat of his brow, food, drink and raiment. Every second of his seventy years is now numbered by the inexorable law of authority, but not the authority of the Pope. Yet he has made no provision for recreation, literature, music, baseball or travel. But the end is not yet.

Turn to human and civil laws. To what extent do these control my life and liberty? We in the United States are smothered in laws: one million, nine hundred thousand of them,[2] and still they pile up, up. All these laws command obedience or send us to jail, and some people are actually doing penance for their disobedience to these laws. To be exact, there are one hundred and twenty-five American citizens in jails to every 100,000 of the population; and what is more to the point, those who keep the laws must pay to jail those who break them.

The authority of the law embodied in men, instruments in God's hands, for God deals with men through men, touches our lives and directs our ways from our coming in to our going out of the world. It touches our daily conduct, our families, our partnerships, our properties, our agreements, insurances, taxes, trades, education, our wills, deaths and fu-

[2] Merle Thrope in *Collier's National Weekly*, Oct. 15, 1927.

nerals. Almost every new day begins with a fresh law
to hem us in.

We must hire official interpreters of these two
million laws, and these lawyers themselves are cir-
cumscribed by law—law—law. So uncertain are the
interpretations and applications of these laws that
different lawyers render contradictory explanations
of the same propositions, so that the happy uncer-
tainty of law becomes thereby a blessing to some, to
others a curse. "Truly nine-tenths of our life is
handed over to the law." Like a shadow it keeps
pace with us from our coming in, even to our going
out of life. The authority of the natural law and
the civil laws has so enveloped us in the "Land of
the Free" that there is precious little of our life left
to give to the Pope. Yet the Pope is successor to
St. Peter and as such has the authority Christ con-
ferred on Peter I. Less or more authority he cannot claim or receive. He never did, never could,
never will claim a particle of civil or political authority from God or from the Constitution of the
Church. He does not claim to be infallible in his
Church policy, when privately interpreting the Bible
or the Church's Constitution, in his letters, counsel
or commands, excommunications or interdicts. He
does not claim to be infallible in his laws or disci-
plines. He does not claim to be inspired, to be without sin, to have the best solution of this or that scientific, political, religious or social problem. Many
of the Popes, as well as many of our United States

Supreme Justices, have published scientific works about political economy, philosophy, history, which have been discarded by other Catholic and American scholars. The fact that the Supreme Justice of the United States has power to define a doctrine of political faith to be held by all American citizens does not make him more virtuous or prudent or sinless than any other citizen in his private capacity. The power of the Supreme Justice to define what is the Law is not given him for his benefit, but for the welfare of all the people. The privilege of infallibility to define what is and what is not the Divine Law, does not change the Pope's character or temperament or weight or height or health or brain. It does not make him inspired or a prophet or sinless. The gift is not for the benefit of the Pope himself, but for the eternal welfare of the faithful.

But please tell us when and how does the Pope claim to be infallible, since he is not infallible as Bishop of Rome, or when he interprets the Laws and Constitutions of the Church privately, or the Scriptures, or when he issues mandates, counsels, excommunications or interdicts, or when he writes on Church government, worship or discipline, or when he expounds science, philosophy, theology or history? God Almighty in the person of Jesus Christ said He would protect Peter and his successors from error when they should declare for the whole world what is or what is not the revealed Law of Jesus Christ. The Vatican Council declared the successor of St. Peter to be protected from error when speaking as Supreme Pastor, he defines a doctrine of faith or morals to be held by the whole Church.

The Pope's definition of a doctrine of faith is not a new revelation. The definition is new, but the revealed truth contained in the definition is as old as Christianity. No one can add, change or subtract one iota of Revelation. Who can improve on Revelation? Can man improve on God? When a Supreme Justice of the United States acting as the organ of the Supreme Court defines a political dogma he does not add to, change or subtract from the Constitution of the United States. The wording of the definition is new, but the truths contained in it are as old as the Constitution. Many of our United States Supreme Justices have published works on law, politics, science and history, and other lawyers and men of learning have attacked or denied their conclusions. But when as Supreme Justice and spokesman for the welfare of the whole nation, he defines a doctrine or policy, that definition is unassailable and is the last Court of Appeal. When Washington has spoken its last word, the case is closed.

Let me give two examples of what I mean. In the year 325 A. D., at the Great Council of Nicæa, the Church declared that Jesus Christ is truly God. This definition was new, but the doctrine was as old as Christianity. The Pope is infallible when he declares what is of Revelation. He does not create it. There can be no new discovery in religion. On a truth of revelation, as upon a dogma of mathematics, time can erect no change. The early Christians believed that Christ is God. One hundred million years will not make God a mere man. Two and two made four in the first century, and the roll of one hundred million years cannot make two and two five. Improvement and progress and evolution have no meaning if applied to perfect things. Years add nothing to God's knowledge. The creature cannot improve on the Creator.

The word "progress," writes the learned Father Phelan, S.J., in his well-known work, THE STRAIGHT PATH, has no meaning when applied to perfect things. "Christ promised that the Spirit of Truth should abide with His Church for ever. "Can she then declare as true in one generation what she brands as false in another? Can God be deceived or can time add to His knowledge? Can man improve on His work? Yes, when he can add fire to the sun, give a richer perfume to the lily or paint the heavens with a deeper blue.

Consequently, when a person boasts of his Church being progressive, he declares that the truths she held yesterday she abandons today, that the truths she holds today she may throw overboard tomorrow. He declares her a man-made Church, a creature of time, a human institution bearing on her forehead the sign of clay.

There are ways in which the Church is very progressive indeed.

She marched not only abreast of but far ahead of her times when she raised humanity out of the mire of pagan corruption into the pure light and freedom of Christian civilization.

But when a portion of mankind revolts from her guidance, breaks down the barriers of moral restraint, reopens the sluice-gates of vice, quenches star after star in the heaven of the soul, and recedes to the paganism from which she rescued it, calling that process "progress," she declines to go on such a journey. She came from above and her motto for mankind must be Excelsior.

In another sense also she is progressive. Her mission is Divine but worked out through human instruments. She used the roads of pagan Rome to expedite the message of her missionaries, and the common language of the Empire to announce it. Today she looks with kindly eye on all inventions and discoveries. Of them she will in the future absorb and utilize all that is good and serviceable. The infidel astronomer now wrapt in his observatory, marking with his telescope the march of the midnight stars, or the scientist now wrestling with the terrors of the polar seas or deciphering the mystic language of the rocks, little dreams that he is strengthening her arm to grapple with the future forces of infidelity, and forging cutting steel for the armory of her defensive weapons.

In this sense she is indeed progressive. But ask her

to vary her articles of faith—change her pillars of belief. "No, never an iota."

In 1925 the Supreme Justice of the United States defined that parents have an inalienable right to educate their children in schools of their choice. This definition was new. The doctrine of parental rights is as old as the Constitution, as old as the human race. The Supreme Court cannot improve on the natural law. To call into doubt this decision and definition of the Supreme Justice of the United States, is to brand yourself anti-American and at enmity with the human family.

The gift of inerrancy granted to the Pope by the Author of Revelation does not change his nature or temperament, or make him more virtuous, learned or protected from human frailty and weakness. The gift is not for the man who fills the high office, but for the guidance of the people on the road to Eternal success. The ceremony of the investiture of the Supreme Justice of the United States does not change his appearance, or his age or weight or height and physical, mental or moral character. The office is not for the man, but exists to aid the people to pursue and overtake happiness. If sinlessness were required of the Pope or the Supreme Justice, as indispensable to his definitions and decisions, there would be no decisions. For who can say when any man is without sin?

If on the other hand God elected an Angel— which He might have done—to render these definitions, we might be tempted to attribute to the superior qualities of the Angel the power of inerrancy. But when God selects the weak things of this world to declare to us His Will, His Power and Wisdom shine forth and when we know we are submitting not to man but to God, the sting is taken from the act of obedience to one of our kind. The free will of man can never be rightfully subjected except to the Will of God. In this case subjection to the will of man becomes by Divine decree identical with subjection to the Will of God Himself. Christ not only taught but practiced this doctrine. In obedience to authority Christ was beyond all doubt the perfect example in history. He obeyed God. He obeyed the civil law. He obeyed man.

But when and how did God confer on the Pope the gift and privilege of inerrancy to declare the law of revelation? When Christ's mission was about to close He called His disciples around Him and asked: "Whom do men say that the Son of Man is? But they said: Some John the Baptist, and other some Elias, and others Jeremias, or one of the prophets. Jesus saith to them: But whom do you say that I am? Simon Peter answered and said: Thou art Christ, the Son of the Living God. And Jesus answering said to him: Blessed art thou, Simon Bar-Jona: because flesh and blood hath not revealed it to thee, but My Father Who is in heaven. And I say to thee: That thou art Peter; and upon this rock I will build My church, and the gates of hell shall not prevail against it. And I will give to thee the keys of the kingdom of heaven. And whatsoever thou shalt bind upon earth, it shall be bound also in heaven: and whatsoever thou shalt loose on earth, it shall be loosed also in heaven." [3]

Christ bestowed on Peter the first Pope a name that is forever a symbol of his office: Rock—not an ordinary one, but a rock of such proportions that it is indestructible.

In adding: "the gates of hell shall not prevail" against the Church founded on Peter the Rock, Christ warned us what the future holds: bloody persecutions in every form from within and without, and in every age, fire, sword, prison, gallows, war; false teachers, false prophets, false science, false brethren, anarchy, schism and tyranny, bigotry and the sword of the persecutor, will, in fact and metaphor, forever be raised over the head of the Church. But God has sworn before heaven and earth: "against my Church the gates of hell shall not prevail." In order to drive home once again into the ear of the world that His Church is a Divine visible organization with a visible head in which all are one, as Father, Son and Holy Ghost, are one in essence in substance, Christ used a metaphor familiar to everyone in His time and in ours: To St. Peter He said: "Feed my lambs; . . . feed my sheep." [4] In Christ's native land the ruler is referred to as a shepherd,

[3] Matthew XVI. 13-19.
[4] John XXI. 16-17.

and his subjects—the flock. Christ, the visible head of the Church, while He lived on earth called Himself "The Good Shepherd," and He appointed St. Peter to lead his flock to healthy pastures and feed them with the bread of life. The Pope after Christ is the visible head of the Church. He is the fountain head of pure doctrine. If the head can teach error; if God allows Satan or his satellites to poison the fountain of truth, the flock is doomed to death. But Christ speaks a final word to Peter, and by this word doubly reassures the Church of His protecting hand. "Simon, Simon! behold Satan hath desired to have you, that he may sift you as wheat: but I have prayed for thee, that thy faith fail not; and thou, being once converted, confirm thy brethren." [5] If Peter could make a mistake in teaching God's Word he will confirm his brethren in error—not in truth.

Now all these words of Christ God mean something. In summary they mean this if anything. Christianity is a revelation. A revelation is a message from God. If the mouthpiece of that revelation—he who is to explain it through all ages—is not infallible, of what earthly use to man is a revelation; of what benefit to mankind? If God has spoken, and if the man appointed to guard His Word can corrupt it, of what use is it for God to speak at all. If God appointed Peter guardian of revelation, that guardian must be infallible. What more signal victory for

[5] Luke XXII. 31-32.

hell than millions of God creatures in Christ's army led astray by the one appointed by God to lead them to victory? Then God has met defeat at the hands of Satan. Hell has triumphed over Heaven.

In our restless, faithless, changing, shifting, uneasy world one supreme guardian, only one in all this world, claims to be the head of a Divine visible organization, and Divinely claims to speak infallibly when he says: "This is what Christ taught, take it or leave it. If you take it, you sacrifice your private opinion to the Word of God. If you reject it, you pit your brain against the mind of God."

By what rule can we evaluate the stupendous claims of the Pope? How do we test any claim of any man? By the measure of time. It is an old saying and a true one: "Time will tell the tale." Since Christ spoke his promises: "I am with you—the gates of hell shall not prevail," twenty centuries have come and nineteen have gone. Let those who do not accept the infallibility of the Pope, as explained by the Church, turn back the pages of history and show us one case where the Pope in his office of Guardian of God's Word failed to announce the truth. Let them show us where he erred. Here is a challenge! The documents containing every infallible definition and decision of the Pope since the beginning are on record. Show me one Pope who has contradicted another when declaring the Law of God. As private individuals the church's worst enemies can point to not more than a dozen whose private lives were not in harmony with their exalted office. Twelve is a small number out of two hundred and sixty-one, when you remember that Christ's own band held one traitor.

As private individuals and in the capacity of scientists, philosophers, historians, theologians or astronomers, some have expounded theories no longer accepted in our generation. Time has proved them as liable to err as any other men when speaking or writing or teaching as private individuals. All the more, on this account, does their privilege of infallibility shine forth when contrasted with their human weakness. But the high character and learning and morality of the Popes as a body, is a matter of historical wonder even to Protestant historians. The history of the Popes is the history of Christian civilization. Thirty Popes have shed their blood to preserve the faith of Jesus Christ and to lay the foundation of the civilization we now enjoy. Seventy-nine are canonized Saints of God. During the Middle Ages there were eighty-one universities in Europe, and fifty-three of these were founded by the Popes. Many of the languages which we now speak the Church first put into writing. No wonder Mr. Gladstone, Protestant statesman, could say: "Her learning is the learning of the world."

Protestants who are accustomed to associate "Catholicism" with "ignorance" should know that the Popes were the patrons of architecture, painting, sculpture, arts and crafts, music, poetry, education,

science, philosophy and ethics. As individual scholars time has proved that they are as liable to be
mistaken in their private scholarship as any other
men. But they have as men a foresight and a prudence which is the result of twenty centuries of experience with the world. For the last four hundred
years the worst enemies of the Church dare not show
a spot or stain on the moral or intellectual character of any of the Popes. In judging the Popes of the
Middle Ages, you must first find out the state of the
world in those barbaric days. This American writers
do not take the trouble to do. Rulers were tyrants
or barbarians. Their subjects were slaves. To sub-
due such men the Popes were not afraid to use strong
measures. By the weapon of the Cross and the sanc-
tions of God's law they subdued tyrants. By Christian education they civilized mankind.

"No one but a master," says Newman: "who
was a thousand bishops in himself at once could have
tamed and controlled as the Pope did the great and
little tyrants of the Middle Ages." "It is impossible
to conceive," wrote Milman: "what had been the
confusion, the lawlessness, the chaotic state of the
Middle Ages without the mediæval Papacy." These
were deeds of the highest service to the future of
mankind. "The right to warn and punish powerful
men, to excommunicate kings, to preach aloud truth
and justice to the inhabitants of the earth, to de-
nounce immoral doctrine, to strike at rebellion in

the garb of heresy, were the very weapons by which Europe was brought into a civilized condition.

No wonder the leaders of the world added to the Pope's other titles that of "Father of European Civilization." [6] Fortunately for us, in the plan of God America was hidden away for fifteen centuries, till mankind had taken its first lessons in Christian Civilization in the Old World. We are heirs to all that was best in European civilization, and Europe owes its civilization to the Popes.

[6] Cardinal Newman: "The Pope," p. 47.

VII

THE PRESIDENT

"Lord of the Universe! Shield us and guide us
Trusting Thee, always through shadow and sun!
Thou hast united us, who will divide us?
Keep us, O keep us, the Many in One."

                                        Holmes.

UNITY is stamped on the Great Seal of the United States: E PLURIBUS UNUM. Unity is written into the dollar. Unity is woven into the fiber of the nation. Like an electric fluid unity runs through all the veins and arteries of the nation from the fountain head, the President. Nowhere on earth, save in the Church, do we find unity in variety so beautifully exemplified as in the United States of America. The sentiment woven in every American heart is Liberty and Union, now and forever, one and inseparable. "We are a sovereign nation of many sovereign states, a perfect union, one and inseparable. One body and one spirit, one President, and one political faith. There is one fold and one Supreme Shepherd. "In necessary things unity; in doubtful things liberty; in all things charity." [1] "With malice toward

[1] St. Augustine.

71

none; with charity towards all." [2] "Let our object be our country, our whole country, and nothing but our country. We have no room in this country," said Roosevelt, "for but one flag, the Stars and Stripes, and we shall follow no allegiance to any other flag whether a foreign flag, or a red flag, or a black flag."

"We the people of the United States." [3] The Nation is sovereign and supreme. "Unity is the source of all national, social and personal happiness." [4] "We must not be enemies. The mystic chords of memory stretching from every battle field and patriot's grave to every loving heart and hearthstone all over this broad land, will swell the chorus of the Union." [5] Lincoln knew that wherever there is the trace of God's finger there is unity: unity in variety. Unity in the planets for they are moved by one central power. Unity in the ocean's ebb and flow, unity in the change of the seasons, in the rising and setting of the sun, unity in every plant and tree and flower.

Unity where there is one God. The President of the United States is the embodiment of the unity of our nation. Twenty-nine Presidents have ruled the nation and sat in the Chair of Washington through one century and a half. The authority which God, by the voice of the people, reposed in Washington runs down the line of Presidents like an electric current to

[2] Lincoln.
[3] The Constitution.
[4] Webster.
[5] Lincoln.

OUR TWENTY-NINE PRESIDENTS

President Coolidge, who holds aloft to the States of the Union, and to the nations of the World, the Light of Liberty. The President of the United States is the symbol of unity. He abhors division, dissension and bigotry, the spirit of intolerance and persecution, for all these are foreign to the Constitution, "the laws and the genius of free men." The President is the visible sign of unity and freedom. But he is not independent. In question of power said Jefferson: "let no more be heard of confidence in man, but bind him down from mischief by the chains of the Constitution."

In the American system of government no room is left for private experiments, opinions or interpretations alien to or foreign to the Constitution. The President is bound by a Solemn Oath of Office to put the Constitution first and himself last. This oath is taken in the presence of the Nation's Chief Justice and of God's primeval representative enthroned in the conscience of the President. This representative of God—is there to applaud, or reprove or condemn, when none other is nigh. Man's conscience is an open book to God. The truer the conscience the more faithful is the office-holder to the duties of his office. Before he enters on the execution of his office the President takes the following oath: "I do solemnly swear that I will faithfully execute the Office of President of the United States, and will to the best of my ability, preserve, protect and defend the Constitution of the United States." "I do solemnly swear!" The essence of an oath consists in calling upon God to witness the truth of what we say. The purpose of the oath is to give greater weight to the words spoken or to the promise made. It is the strongest guarantee we can evoke from the lips of mortal man. He who exacts the oath, he who takes it, and the nation that listens to it, make an act of faith in God. To appeal to God is to acknowledge Him the highest and best in all things. It is an acknowledgment of God's truth and justice and holiness.

"And thou shalt swear: as the Lord liveth, in truth, and in judgment, and in justice." [6] Thou shalt swear in truth. What we promise and what we swear to, we must sincerely purpose to perform to the best that is within us. To swear a false oath is to commit perjury, punishable in this life and in the next. A promise taken under oath with the intention of not fulfilling it is equally criminal. It is the solemn teaching of the Church that perjury and a false oath are mortal sins, that is, a deliberate violation of a commandment of God in a grave matter. By this sin God is solemnly renounced, His sanctity, justice and omniscience are mocked and His vengeance is called down upon the offender.

The sanctity of the oath is one of the cherished teachings of the Church. It was taught and preserved, protected and defended, for eighteen hundred years before Washington raised his hand and in presence of God swore: "to preserve, protect and

[6] Jeremias IV. 2.

defend the Constitution of the United States." It is to teach the sanctity of the oath as part of the program of religious instruction that Catholics pour out their last penny to build and maintain schools, colleges and universities all over this land, and all over the world; while at the same time they pay their full share of taxes for the support of public institutions. This does not imply that our public institutions of learning teach the contrary, but that the subject of religion is omitted from their program of studies.

The Courts of the land are the people's tribunals of Justice. The sanctity of the oath is the foundation of the Court. The history of the Church is filled with instances of Catholics going cheerfully to death rather than violate the dictates of conscience. This will explain too the spontaneity of Catholic patriotism. When the Nation's Leaders called Catholics were among the first in the field and the last to quit. This explains why in one hundred and fifty years of life, Uncle Sam could say: "Among the Catholic citizens no Arnold can be found."

We have set side by side the two institutions which Mr. Evans, super-President of America, and Senator Heflin, his foreign representative at Washington, maintain are in direct conflict: The Papacy and the Presidency.

Are the two rails of a railroad in conflict with each other, because they run parallel to each other?

Is Mr. Evans' eye in conflict with his nose, because both are in the same head?

The Church is spoken of in Scripture as a "body," a "Kingdom," a "sheepfold," a "house," a "Temple," a "tree." "And He hath subjected all things under His feet, and hath made Him head over all the Church, which is His body.[7] "When anyone heareth the Word of the Kingdom of God." [8] "And other sheep I have, that are not of this fold; them also I must bring, and they shall hear My voice, and there shall be one fold and one shepherd." [9] "Be you also as living stones built up, a Spiritual house." [10] "Know you not that you are the temple of God, and that the Spirit of God dwelleth in you?" [11] "The kingdom of heaven is like to a grain of mustard seed . . . which is the least indeed of all seeds; but when it is grown up . . . and becometh a tree, so that the birds of the air come, and dwell in the branches thereof." [12]

The Sacred writers used these metaphors and figures of speech to stamp on the mind Christ's idea of one visible organization, united in one visible head, the Pope. The same idea is copied into the formation of our American government. Every patriot from Washington to Coolidge reiterated over and over the idea of one nation under one head. We had an example in the Civil War of the horrors of a family with two Fathers, a Nation with two Presi-

[7] Ephes. I. 22-23.
[8] Matthew XIII. 19.
[9] John X. 16.
[10] I. Peter II. 5.
[11] I. Cor. III. 16.
[12] Matthew XIII. 31-32.

dents, a house divided against itself. The results are too unpleasant to recall. The Church is of every nation but one all over the earth.

As the members of the human body are directed and governed by but one head, so in the Church and in the United States. What is it that cements the individual members of the Church into one spiritual edifice? Unity of faith and unity of government. The government of America extends its blessings equally to all the States of the Union under one supreme head, the President. The Constitution of the United States binds the President, as the Pope is bound by the Laws of God and the Constitution of the Church. We cannot believe in Americanism, unless we believe in the President. We should not believe in the Church, unless we believe in its visible head, the Pope.

The union of all nations in the Church may be likened to a great monument where every variety of marble and material on earth find a fitting place, all resting on the immovable rock, Peter. The union of all people in the forty-eight States of America with their President, each contributing something distinct to the whole, presents a picture of unity in variety. Roosevelt expressed this thought when he said: "Let us keep our pride in the stocks from which we have sprung, but let us show our pride by joining in a spirit of generous rivalry to see which can do most for our great common country—we are all Americans."

Now if the Presidency and the Papacy are in conflict, there would be in one hundred and fifty years some instances on record from the pen of the Popes or Presidents. In one hundred and fifty years there were twenty-nine Presidents and ten Popes. Has the Pope ever complained that American Catholics were not loyal to his spiritual leadership? On the contrary, the Popes have repeatedly praised the spiritual loyalty of American Catholics. What have the twenty-nine Presidents said about the civil allegiance of Catholics? They have each and all sung the praises of Catholics in peace and war. Some one has said that people who try to be more Catholic than the Pope and more American than the President are suffering from a chronic attack of "nerves." They see visions and dream dreams. Their place is in the psychopathic ward. That disease is beyond the practice of the family physician. The specialists ought to be consulted.

The natural rule by which we test the value of any idea or statement is time. If the Pope has ever meddled in the politics of the United States since its birth, we ask you as a special favor to point it out to us. If you have any special data on this vital question Catholics should know of it. And if Catholics know of any expression from the mouth of the Presidents which might remove prejudice, non-Catholics should know of it. "For nothing is grander than to break the chains of ignorance, to destroy the phantoms of the soul."

Here are a few expressions of Great Presidents:

WASHINGTON

"It is the duty to address public thanks to our Catholic brethren, as to them we are indebted for every late success over the common enemy in Canada."

Nov. 5, 1775.

When Washington was elected President, the Catholics presented him with an address in which they said:

"This prospect of national prosperity is peculiarly pleasing to us on another account, because, whilst our country preserves her freedom and independence, we shall have a well-founded title to claim from her justice, the equal rights of citizenship, as the price of our blood spilt under your eyes, and of our common exertions for her defense, under your auspicious conduct, rights rendered more dear to us by the remembrance of former hardships. When we pray for the preservation of them, where they have been granted—and expect the full extension of them from the justice of those States which still restrict them—when we solicit the protection of heaven over our common country, we neither omit, nor can omit, recommending your preservation to the singular care of Divine Providence."

To this Washington replied:

"As mankind becomes more liberal, they will be more apt to allow that all those who conduct themselves as worthy members of the community are equally entitled to the protection of the civil government. I hope ever to see America among the foremost nations in examples of justice and liberality. And I presume that your fellow citizens will not forget the patriotic part which you took in the accomplishment of their Revolution and the establishment of your government; or the important assistance which they received from a nation in which the Roman Catholic faith is professed."

JEFFERSON

"All and every act of parliament by whatever title known or distinguished, which renders criminal the maintaining of any opinions in matters of religion . . . or exercising any mode of worship whatever . . . shall henceforth be of no validity or force within this Commonwealth."

Statute of Virginia for Religious Freedom.

MADISON

"That diabolical, hell-conceived principle of persecution rages among us. I have neither patience to hear, talk or think of anything relative to this matter; for I have squabbled and scolded, abused and ridiculed so long about it to little purpose, that I am without common patience."

Statement made two years before Virginia Constitutional Convention.

LINCOLN

"When the Know-Nothings get control, it (the Declaration) will read "All men are created equal except negroes, foreigners and Catholics." When it comes to this I should prefer emigrating to some country where they make no pretense of loving liberty."

Letter to Joshua F. Speed. 1855.

ROOSEVELT

"Any political movement directed against any body of our fellow citizens because of their religious creed is a grave offense against American principles and American institutions."

Oct. 11, 1915.

TAFT

"There is nothing so despicable as a secret society that is based upon religious prejudice and that will attempt to defeat a man because of his religious beliefs. Such a society is like a cockroach—it thrives in the dark. So do those who combine for such an end."

Dec. 20, 1914.

WILSON

"It does not become America that within her borders, where every man is free to follow the dictates of his conscience, men should raise the cry of church against church. To do that is to strike at the spirit and heart of America."

Nov. 4, 1915.

HARDING

"In the experiences of a year of the presidency, there has come to me no other such unwelcome impression as the manifest religious intolerance which exists among many of our citizens. I hold it to be a menace to the very liberties we boast and cherish."

March 24, 1922.

In this statement the President has direct reference to the usurping government of the Klan. For millions of citizens the oath of allegiance was not to the President of the United States but to the usurping President of the Klan:

"I, in the presence of God and man swear unconditionally that I will faithfully obey the constitution and laws and will willingly conform to all regulations, usages and requirements of the Ku Klux Klan which now exist or may be hereafter enacted, and will render at all times loyal and steadfast support to the imperial authority of same and will hereby heed all official mandates, decrees, edicts, rulings and instructions of the Imperial Wizard therein."

There is no room here for our President, our Constitution or Declaration of Independence. The citizens who left America for this Klan Empire so grieved the heart of President Harding as to force him to declare: "they are a menace to our country." Listen to a Protestant scholar and gentleman, The Hon. Aldrich Blake, describe this "menace to our country":

About four years ago, the Ku Klux Klan stole silently into Oklahoma. Scarcely anyone was aware of its arrival. Six months later it had developed the velocity of a hurricane and the madness of a maniac. By the spring of 1921, no man's business, no man's employment, no man's life was safe unless he belonged to the Invisible Empire. Social moorings, which had withstood the strain of war, suddenly snapped, and in a short time Oklahoma was a land of broken friendships and broken hearts—a vast field of social chaos lighted only by the glare of the fiery cross. The wounds are still fresh; the sores are still open; not until the new generation matures will Oklahoma fully recover from her orgy.

It will require a decade to repair the mortal damage inflicted alone by the Klan policy of deception, a fact indelibly impressed upon my mind at the first hearings of the military tribunal at Tulsa. A witness is sworn; the examination begins:

"Do you belong to the Klan?"

"No, sir."

"Have you ever belonged?"

"No, sir."

"Have you ever paid dues to the Ku Klux Klan or been in the Klan hall?"

"No, sir."

"Have you ever seen one of these?"

"No, sir," is the answer as the witness examines a Klan membership card.

"Officer, search the witness!"

Not once, but several times in the early stages of the investigation, a Klan card was extracted from the witness' pocket by an attaché of the court. Soon, for some reason, Klansmen left their cards at home, so they could commit perjury with less danger of detection, is the only possible conclusion.

The effect upon civic standards of teaching thousands to make mendacity a virtue, I leave to the conjecture of those Christian ministers who have mistaken the fiery cross for "the cross of Him who died on the crest of a Syrian hill for the salvation of the race."

There is one group of citizens who have never in one hundred and fifty years—and who never shall while the Republic endures—cause any president to say: "They are a menace to our country." These are citizens who profess the Catholic Faith. America will have nothing to fear but everything good to hope from the Catholic Church. The great American statesman and financier Mark Hanna said:

"I lay my head on my pillow every night with more satisfaction because I know there is in our midst a great conservative element in the Catholic Church."

To make amends in some way for the insults daily heaped on his head by ungrateful children, the President of the United States is comforted by the fact that from the hearts of 25,000 priests, 33,990 nuns and religious, and 19,689,049 Catholics, the Church's prayer for the President goes up to God:

"We ask the blessing of God for our President and for all in high station that they may lead a quiet and holy life, for peace and good will among all states and peoples and for the necessities of mankind."

VIII

THE VATICAN AND THE WHITE HOUSE

"Great dynasties die like the flowers of the field.
Great empires wither and fall;
Glories there have been that blazed to the stars
They have been—and that is all.
But there is the grand old Roman See
The ruins of earth among
Young with the youth of its early prime
With the strength of Peter strong."

Murry.

THE Vatican at Rome is to the Universal Church what the Capitol at Washington is to the United States. The Pope lives at the Vatican. In his sphere —marked out to him by Christ—he is to some 330,-000,000 Catholics of the world what the President is in his sphere to 120,000,000 citizens of the United States.

Because the first Pope's name was Peter, that is Rock, the greatest Basilica in the world St. Peter's at Rome, is built and named after him. In Rome St. Peter labored and died, and like his Master, was crucified. It was fitting that the center of universal unity should be built over his tomb. The Church, too, needed the Roman law and Roman language to spread the faith, so that the ancient capital of the ancient Empire became the logical center of the everlasting Christian Church: Rome, where a million martyrs died!

Washington was first President of the United States. It was fitting that the visible center of unity should be named after him. Rome has the last word in the government of the Church, and is often referred to as the Church. We have the motto: "Rome has spoken, the case is finished." We are wont to speak of our government as "Washington." When Washington speaks all must listen. Washington is the center of unity, the White House of the President; the heart of the nation. To Washington every national concern must go to receive the stamp of the nation. Where Washington is there is America. For more than 330,000,000 Catholics the last Court of Appeal in religious matters is Rome. "Where Peter is there is the Church." [1]

Washington belongs to no State of the Union. It is extraterritorial—the District of Columbia. This leaves the President free and secure from the obligations of any particular State. The President is not a citizen of any of the States. "I have not a sectional bone in my body," said President Roosevelt. The Pope is not a citizen of any Italian state—or of any state in the world. The laws and civil jurisdiction of Italy or Rome do not obtain in the Vatican. The Vatican and all it embraces enjoy immunity, and are

[1] St. Ambrose.

extraterritorial. All actions of the Italian authority or any other authority stop at the Gates of the Vatican, and this is not according to Italian Law only but International Law as well. A spiritual chief whose jurisdiction extends to every portion of the earth, whose subjects are of every race and clime and tongue must not be under the influence of any foreign power, but free, free to tell all men, even rulers: "Do Penance for the Kingdom of Heaven is at hand." [2]

With just pride we citizens point to the glorious traditions built around the city of Washington in the short span of one hundred and fifty years. It has a history and a glory which with the passing of years grows more sacred to the heart of the true American. Catholics point with pride to Rome—center of Spiritual Authority, from the very foundation of the Church. About ten years after the death of Christ Peter made Rome his home, and the center of his operations. What did Peter meet at Rome? Let the historian answer:

"A people whose superb intellect, indomitable character and implacable power were in every phase of religious, intellectual, moral, social and political life absolutely opposed to the doctrine that he taught and the law that he upheld."

What did Rome adore? "Her ideal of civilization was Saturn—a cannibal who devoured his own children. Her ideal of pleasure was Bacchus—a drunk-

[2] Matthew II. 17.

ard. Her ideal of work was Vulcan—a cripple. Her ideal of wisdom was Minerva—a virago. Her ideal of wit was Mercury—a thief. Her ideal of woman-hood was Diana—a maiden without chastity, a hunt-ress without a heart, or it was Venus the beautiful, a creature without shame. Rome's king of the gods was Jupiter an abandoned profligate." To these things Rome built temples, offered incense and poured out prayer. The historians Seneca, Suetonius, Juvenal and Tacitus sum up Rome's moral condition in the motto: "to corrupt, and to be corrupted." In the words of Renan: "Rome under the Cæsars was a very Hell." Against this Peter arrayed himself. One old man against Rome's temples, her court, her senate and her camp. But Peter said he was Christ's Vicar on earth; that he would replace the eagle by the Cross.

Now Rome owned the earth. Rome made war on Peter. It lasted three hundred years, till Peter and twenty-nine of his successors were martyred. These were the centuries of blood, and Rome's motto was: "The Christians to the lions!" St. Peter came to Rome about the year 30 A.D. and died in 55 A.D. The Roman Caius who lived in the second century wrote to Proclus: "But I can show you the trophies of the Apostles. If you care to go to the Vatican or to the Road to Ostia, thou shalt find the trophies (tombs) of those who founded this Church." [3]

The Primacy of Peter was unquestioned. While

[3] Robert J. Kane, S. J.: Lecture "From Peter to Leo."

St. John the Evangelist was still living, disputes arose among the Christians of Corinth. The matter was referred not to St. John, one of the twelve apostles, not to the congregations or elders, but to Pope Clement I of Rome, St. Peter's successor. In the beginning of the second century St. Irenæus wrote: "On account of the supremacy of Rome, it is necessary that the faithful everywhere should be in communion with it." Cyprian wrote in 258 A.D.: "To the Church of Rome heresy can have no access." In 343 the Council of Sardica declared: "that it is best and most fitting to have recourse to the Head that is to the See of Peter." In the fourth century St. Augustine wrote to St. Ambrose: "Rome has spoken, the case is ended." "Where Peter is there is the Church." [4] The Primacy of Peter and his successors is, like the Primacy of Washington and his successors an indisputable historical fact. "If you are Christians you are Romans." [5]

"It is the law of the Church that at stated periods every bishop in the world must visit Rome and report to the Pope on the condition of his diocese. One year is set for the bishops of one country, and another year for the bishops of another. Thus there is a constant procession of the governors of the Church over the threshold of the Apostles, as messengers hastening from the field of battle bearing tidings to their chief of the fortunes of the war.

[4] St. Ambrose.
[5] St. Patrick's "Confessions."

As that lonely prisoner in his own palace sits clad all in white by the tomb of the fisherman and listens to their varied messages, what a world panorama must he gaze on—what ever-changing pictures of hope and fear, of joy and sorrow, of victory and defeat. Here, with ashes on their heads and garments reeking with the odor of the prison, come the envoys of Russia with their sad story, even in this twentieth century, of Cossack brutality, of the knout and the exile and the heavy chains. To them succeeds some maimed and scarred veteran of the Far East, to tell the old tale of how a new Chinese riot has proved for the thousandth time the old story that the generation of Good Shepherds is ever renewed in the Church, who know how to lay down their lives for their sheep. From Spain come disquieting rumors of war; and lest any bitterness should be wanting to his chalice, there run along the walls the stealthy whisperings of traitors within the gates.

But there is another footstep upon the threshold, and already another spirit in the air. Who are they that come robed, indeed, in the ancient Roman purple, but with the wine of youth in their veins? From far beyond the seas, from the uttermost parts of the earth they hasten—the bearers of tidings of great joy. From Canada, from the Cape, from Australia, from our own United States, they bring consolation to the Father of Christendom in his bitter hour. They tell of new nations that build in new

lands innumerable altars to the God who has glad-
dened their youth. They tell of the wise work of the
pioneers, the noble generosity of the faithful, the
good report with those that are without. Dioceses
are erected, parishes formed, churches built, schools
founded, all the works of mercy multiplied. The
Holy Mass is attended, the Sacraments are fre-
quented, the young are instructed, the sick visited,
and the poor have the gospel preached to them. Sta-
tistics are unreliable and numbers vain, but what
can equal the eloquence of the one fact that in the
United States alone, in the course of four genera-
tions, the number of Sisters devoted to charity and
education has so grown that now it is double the total
Catholic population at the time of the Declaration
of Independence?

When, therefore, we find among men an institution that is dowered with the eternal years, that,
as it were naturally, renews the ravages of time;
that is independent of the vicissitudes of men and
nations; that is killed and yet lives; that is buried
yet walks abroad; that is cast out yet returns to win
the children of the persecutors: what can we be re-
minded of except that Divine Society which we know
that Jesus Christ established and to which He gave
the promise: "Behold I am with you all days, even
to the consummation of the world?" *

At regular intervals the Senators of the United
States bring tidings of joy and sorrow, trial and

* Rev. P. C. Yorke: "The Secular Conflict."

triumph to our President at Washington. He receives them as a kind father, and praises or rebukes them through his encyclical letters. As one in supreme authority he calls us back to the path of truth, to the teachings and dogmas of the Constitution and the glorious heritage of freedom handed down from each of the twenty-eight Presidents who sat in the Chair of Washington. About 120,000,000 citizens render to the President the same fealty which the first citizens gave Washington at the First Constitutional Convention. More than 330,000,000 [7] Catholics tender to the Pope the same spiritual loyalty the early Christians tendered St. Peter when he presided over the First Council of the Church.

Two hundred and sixty Popes have succeeded to the Chair of St. Peter. "Of them, nearly one-third were saints: all of them for over three hundred years martyrs. Their history is the history of civilization, of waiting that was prudent, of progress that was wise. It is a recurring record of the advance of mind against materialism, of order against anarchy, of truth against skepticism. It is a chronicle of the success of freedom over slavery, of kindness over cruelty, of noble ideals over human depravity. Of them all, not one that did not brave the troubled waters of a hostile world. Many of them at the time were supposed to have been hopelessly shipwrecked; but the bark of Peter did not sink, and Peter the

[7] The World Almanac for 1928 gives number of Catholics in the world as 331,000,000.

fisherman, looks and listens as he had listened and looked before. Wave after wave, generation after generation, century after century, comes with its threats and peril and shock, but the centuries pass, and Peter remains. Men overwhelm him by force, or buffet him with insult, laugh at him for his antiquated ways, or howl down his warnings. But men come and pass, while Peter remains the same, the fisherman. Weather-worn, war-worn, world-worn, Peter, the fisherman, looks and listens. He has seen and heard all before. All that is human. But he has also seen a face and heard a voice that is Divine—when standing by the Galilean shore, Jesus said: "Thou art Peter." [8]

In truth, no one may lay claim to a liberal education who has not studied the claims of the See of Rome. Every one knows or ought to know by heart the following passage of the great Protestant writer, Lord Macaulay, in his Essay on "Ranke's History of the Popes":

"There is not, and there never was on this earth, a work of human policy so well deserving of examination as the Roman Catholic Church. The history of that Church joins together the two great ages of human civilization. . . . The proudest royal houses are but of yesterday, when compared with the line of the Supreme Pontiffs. That line we trace back in unbroken series from the Pope who crowned Napoleon in the nineteenth century to the Pope who crowned Pepin in the eighth; and far beyond the time of Pepin the

[8] Rev. Robert J. Kane, S. J.: "From Peter to Leo."

august dynasty extends. . . . The republic of Venice came
next in antiquity. But the republic of Venice was modern
when compared with the Papacy; and the republic of Venice
is gone, and the Papacy remains. The Papacy remains, not
in decay, not a mere antique, but full of life and youthful
vigor. The Catholic Church is still sending forth to the far-
thest ends of the world missionaries as zealous as those who
landed in Kent with Augustine, and still confronting hostile
kings with the same spirit with which she confronted Attila.
. . . Nor do we see any sign which indicates that the term
of her long dominion is approaching. She saw the commence-
ment of all the ecclesiastical establishments that now exist
in the world; and we feel no assurance that she is not
destined to see the end of them all. . . . It is not strange
that, in the year 1799, even sagacious observers should
have thought that, at length, the hour of the Church of
Rome was come. An infidel power ascendant, the Pope
dying in captivity, the most illustrious prelates of France
living in a foreign country on Protestant alms, the noblest
edifices which the munificence of former ages had consecrated to the worship of God turned into Temples of Victory, or into banqueting houses for political societies. . . .
But the end was not yet. . . . Anarchy had had its day. A
new order of things rose out of the confusion, new dynasties,
new laws, new titles; and amidst them emerged the ancient
religion. The Arabs have a fable that the Great Pyramid
was built by antediluvian kings, and alone, of all the works
of men, bore the weight of the flood. Such as this was the
fate of the Papacy. It had been buried under the great inun-
dation; but its deep foundations had remained unshaken;
and, when the waters abated, it appeared alone amidst the
ruins of a world that had passed away. The republic of

Holland was gone, and the empire of Germany, and the great Council of Venice, and the old Helvetian League, and the House of Bourbon, and the parliaments and aristocracy of France. Europe was full of young creations, a French empire, a kingdom of Italy, a Confederation of the Rhine. Nor had the late events affected only territorial limits and political institutions. The distribution of property, the composition and spirit of society, had, through a great part of Catholic Europe, undergone a complete change. But the unchangeable Church was still there." [9]

Mr. Chesterton has said that if there were no Pope it would be necessary to create one; that society will always try to set up some moral power that cannot be reached by material powers. And he is convinced that as people come closer together the necessity for some such international and neutral power becomes imperative. International society needs a moral power that will stand above and beyond all self-seeking, a power that cannot be bought by a compromise. Men will not trust other people's political leaders, emperors or representatives in any World Court or International League. Only through an international moral power can international justice come.

Does this necessity explain why today, after a horrible war and an atrocious peace, thirty-four nations have accredited representatives at the Vatican? The governments of the world go to the Vatican today for help that they can get nowhere else. They

[9] Essay on Ranke's "History of the Popes."

know that the Vatican will always mete out impartial justice. The Holy See is to the world not only the center of an international religion, one and the selfsame in every corner of the earth, but it is a central office for the benefit of human society as a whole. It provides a means of intercourse for those who cannot or will not carry on direct relations with one another. The Vatican with her twenty centuries of experience provides a center firmly fixed on immemorial principles of order and right.

President Wilson knew the power of such an office "to prevent the terrible war from happening again." Some such impartial power for justice he had in mind when he fathered the League of Nations. But after ten years of its existence the League is now referred to in some quarters as "a league of liars and robbers." The Pope, the moral leader of Christendom, the absolute absence of force, was not invited to the peace travesty of Versailles or Geneva, because certain statesmen and philosophers had boasted that science had excommunicated CHRIST from the Parliament of Nations and the affairs of the world. . . .

What has been the public conduct of the rank and file of Catholics in word and work, in peace and war toward the American Republic? Has our practice been in harmony with our theories? Facts speak louder than words. At the opening of the War of Independence Father John Carroll—of the family

of Carrolls that donated the site for the White
House—was delegated by Mr. Franklin to concili-
ate Canada and secure her neutrality. What did the
Pope think of Father Carroll's patriotism? Was he
jealous? The fact is that the Pope made him first
Archbishop of Baltimore and of the entire Catholic
Church in America. During the war with Mexico
President Polk enlisted into his secret corps Bishop
Hughes and thanked him for his counsel and ser-
vice. How did the Pope look on such acts of patriot-
ism? He made Bishop Hughes Archbishop of New
York. In the Civil War Catholic bishops and priests
were the confidants of generals on both sides but the
Pope was neutral. What did the Confederacy think
of the Pope? The Confederate President was Mr.
Davis, a Protestant, his Secretary of State, Mr.
Judah Benjamin a Jew, and his plenipotentiary Mr.
Dudley Mann a Mason. Were these men in doubt
about the patriotism of Catholics or the attitude of
the Pope? Let us see if they were frightened by the
great Protestant tradition. In direct need, in sore
trouble whom do we take to our bosom, to whom do
we confide the secrets of our hearts? In that hour
we search among thousands, aye millions for men
who are true and tried, men who are grit to the core.
And President Davis advised his Secretary of State
to solicit the services of Father Bannon, Chaplain
of the gallant Missourians under General Price to
join his secret service corps and proceed to Europe
in the interests of peace. Six months later President

Davis enlisted the services of Bishop Patrick Lynch
of Charleston, S. C., and entrusted him with the
secrets of the Southland and the Confederacy in
his mission to Europe. Bishop Lynch was in this
capacity the President's other self. And what was
the attitude of the Holy Father Pius IX toward the
South? Listen to Mr. Dudley Mann who appeared
in person before the Holy Father at the Vatican:

Hon. J. P. Benjamin, Secretary of State of the Confederate States of America, Richmond, Va.

Sir:

At three o'clock on the afternoon of yesterday I received
a formal notification that His Holiness would favor me
with an audience embracing my private secretary today at
twelve o'clock. I accordingly proceeded to the Vatican sufficiently early to enable me to reach there fifteen minutes in
advance of the designated hour. In five minutes afterwards,
ten minutes prior to the appointed time, a message came
from the Sovereign Pontiff that he was ready to receive me,
and I was accordingly conducted within his presence.

His Holiness stated, after I had taken my stand near to
his side, that he had been so afflicted by the horrors of the
war in America that many months ago he had written to
the Archbishops of New Orleans and New York to use all
the influence that they could properly employ for terminat-
ing with as little delay as possible the deplorable state of
hostilities; that from the former he had received no answer,
but that he had heard from the latter, and his communica-
tion was not such as to inspire hopes that his ardent wishes
would be speedily gratified. I then remarked: "It is to a
sense of profound gratitude of the Executive of the Con-

federate States and of my countrymen for the earnest manifestations which your Holiness made in the appeal referred to that I am indebted for the distinguished honor which I now enjoy. President Davis has appointed me Special Envoy to convey in person to your Holiness this letter, which I trust you will receive in a similar spirit to that which animated its author." Looking for a moment at the address, His Holiness took his scissors and cut the envelope. Upon opening it he observed: "I see it is in English, a language which I do not understand." I remarked: "If it will be agreeable to your Holiness, my secretary will translate its contents to you." He replied: "I shall be pleased if he will do so." The translation was rendered in a slow, solemn, and emphatic pronunciation. During its progress I did not cease for an instant to carefully survey the features of the Sovereign Pontiff. A sweeter expression of pious affection, of tender benignity, never adorned the face of mortal man. No picture can adequately represent him when exclusively absorbed in Christian contemplation. Every sentence of the letter appeared to sensibly affect him. At the conclusion of each he would lay his hand down upon the desk and bow his head approvingly. When the passage was reached wherein the President states in such sublime and affecting language, "We have offered up at the footstool of our Father who art in heaven prayers inspired by the same feelings which animated your Holiness," his deep-sunken orbs, visibly moistened, were upturned toward that throne upon which ever sits the Prince of Peace, indicating that his heart was pleading for our deliverance from that ceaseless and merciless war which is prosecuted against us. The soul of infidelity, if indeed infidelity have a soul, would have melted in view of so sacred a spectacle. The emotion occasioned by the translation was succeeded by a silence of some time. At length, His Holiness asked me whether President Davis were a Catholic. I answered in the negative. He then asked if I were one. I assured him that I was not.

His Holiness then said: "I should like to do anything that can be effectively done or that even promises good results, to aid in putting an end to this most terrible war which is harming the good of all the earth, if I knew how to proceed."

His Holiness then observed: "I will write a letter to President Davis, and of such a character that it may be published for general perusal." I expressed my heartfelt gratification for the assertion of this purpose. He then remarked, half inquiringly: "You will remain here for several months?" I of course could not do otherwise than answer in the affirmative. Turning to my secretary, he asked several kind questions personal to himself, and bestowed upon him a handsome compliment. He then extended his hand, as a signal for the end of the audience, and I retired. Thus terminated one among the most remarkable conferences that ever a foreign representative had with a potentate of the earth. And such a potentate! A potentate who wields the consciences of 175,000,000 of the civilized race, and who is adored by that immense number as the vicegerent of Almighty God in his sublunary sphere.

How strikingly majestic the conduct of the Government of the Pontifical State in its bearing toward me when contrasted with the sneaking subterfuges to which some of the Governments of western Europe have had recourse in order to evade intercourse with our Commissioners! Here I was openly received at the Department of Foreign Affairs, openly received by appointment at court in accordance with established usages and customs, and treated from beginning to end with a consideration which might be envied by the Envoy of the oldest member of the family of nations. The audience was of forty minutes' duration, an unusually long one.

I have written this despatch very hurriedly, and fear that it will barely be in time for the monthly steamer which goes off from Liverpool with the mails of the Bahama Islands next Saturday.

I have the honor to be, sir, very respectfully, your obedient servant,

A. Dudley Mann.[10]

The letter from the Pope is as follows. Mr. Mann says of this letter to the President: "It will adorn the archives of our country in all coming time."

ILLUSTRIOUS AND HONORABLE SIR, GREETING:

We have lately received with all kindness, as was meet, the gentleman sent by your Excellency to present to us your letter dated on the 23d of last September. We have received certainly no small pleasure in learning, both from these gentlemen and from your letter, the feeling of gratification and of very warm appreciation with which you, illustrious and honorable sir, were moved, when you first had knowledge of our letter written in October of the preceding year to the venerable brethren, John, Archbishop of New York, and John, Archbishop of New Orleans, in which we again and again urged and exhorted those venerable brethren that, because of their exemplary piety and

[10] Messages and Papers of the Confederacy. Vol. II. (Richardson.)

episcopal zeal, they should employ their most earnest effort in our name also, in order that the fatal civil war which had arisen in the States should end, and that the people of America might again enjoy mutual peace and concord, and love each other with mutual charity. And it has been very gratifying to us to recognize, illustrious and honorable sir, that you and your people are animated by the same desire for peace and tranquillity which we had so earnestly inculcated in our aforesaid letter to the venerable brethren above named. O, that the other people also of the States and their rulers, considering seriously how cruel and how deplorable is this intestine war, would receive and embrace the counsels of peace and tranquillity. We shall not cease with most fervent prayers to beseech God, the Best and Highest, and to implore him to pour out the spirit of Christian love and peace upon all the people in America, and to rescue them from the great calamities with which they are afflicted, and we also pray the same most merciful Lord that he will illumine your Excellency with the light of his divine grace, and unite you with ourselves in perfect charity.

Given at Rome, at St. Peters, on the 3d December, 1863, in the eighteenth of our Pontificate.

Pius P. P. IX.[11]

Soon after the Civil War Bishop Gibbons of Richmond proclaimed from his pulpit and platform his love for the United States and the duties of citizens to all civil authority and the happy arrangement of a free Church in a free State. The same Pius IX

[11] Messages and papers of the Confederacy. Vol. II. (Richardson.)

made him Archbishop of Baltimore and Metropolitan of the American Church. But Archbishop Gibbons was not content to preach American democracy in the United States only, but when he was invited to Rome, in the presence of Leo XIII he eulogized the Constitution of the United States and the rapid prosperity of the Church because of the separation of Church and State: and the Pope gave him the highest gift within his power: he created him a Cardinal of the Church. To this great Catholic citizen a monument is now to be erected which will grace the square in front of the White House with those of Lafayette, Rochambeau and Kosciusko—the four horsemen of American patriotism.

But all this looks like ancient history compared with the glorious record of the Catholic Church in America in the late World War. In April, 1917, President Wilson issued the Proclamation of War. The next day the Cardinals and Archbishops of the United States wrote the President:

"Mr. President: Standing firmly upon solid Catholic tradition and history from the very foundation of this nation, we reaffirm in this hour of stress and trial our most sacred and sincere loyalty and patriotism toward our country, our government, and our flag.

"Moved to the very depths of our hearts by the stirring appeal of the President of the United States and by the action of our national congress, we accept whole-heartedly and unreservedly the decree of that legislative authority proclaiming this country to be in a state of war.

"We have prayed that we might be spared the dire necessity of entering the conflict. But now that war has been declared we bow in obedience to the summons to bear our part in it, with fidelity, with courage and with the spirit of sacrifice, which as loyal citizens we are bound to manifest for the defense of the most sacred rights and the welfare of the whole nation.

"Acknowledging gladly the gratitude we have always felt for the protection of our spiritual liberty and the freedom of our Catholic institutions under the flag, we pledge our devotion and our strength to the maintenance of our country's glorious leadership in those possessions and principles which have been America's proudest boast.

"Inspired neither by hate nor fear, but by the holy sentiments of truest patriotic fervor and zeal, we stand ready, we and all the flock committed to our keeping, to co-operate in every way possible with our President and our national government, to the end that the great and holy cause of liberty may triumph, and that our beloved country may emerge from this hour of test stronger and nobler than ever.

"Our people now, as ever, will rise as one man to serve the nation. Our priests and consecrated women will once again, as in every former trial of our country, win, by their bravery, their heroism and their service, new admiration and approval.

"We are all true Americans, ready as our age, our ability and our condition permit, to do whatever is in us to do, for the preservation, the progress and the triumph of our beloved country.

"May God direct and guide our President and our government, that out of this trying crisis in our national life may at length come a closer union among all the citizens of America, and that an enduring and blessed peace may crown the sacrifices which war inevitably entails."

No wonder the President's heart was thrilled and warmed by this expression of loyalty! We are not surprised that the grateful President expressed his appreciation of this so heartily in the following note to Cardinal Gibbons:

"The very remarkable resolutions unanimously adopted by the Archbishops of the United States at their annual meeting in the Catholic University on April 18, last, a copy of which you were kind enough to send me, warms my heart and makes me very proud indeed that men of such large influence should act in so large a sense of patriotism and so admirable a spirit of devotion to our common country."

Not only President Wilson, but other high officials express their appreciation of this declaration of loyalty. A. Mitchell Palmer, Attorney-General of the United States, said:

"I have read with deep interest the Pastoral Letter of the Archbishops and Bishops to their clergy and people of the Catholic Church in the United States, the first that has been issued in the past thirty-five years, and was impressed with its profound thought and lofty tone.

"The greeting from the dignitaries of the Church addressed to their people, not only as members of the Catholic Church, but as citizens of the Republic.

"I am glad that the Catholic Church in the United States, as exemplified by the Pastoral Letter, is showing such splendid and progressive spirit."

How did the Catholic young men answer:

> "We are coming Father Wilson
> Eight hundred sixty thousand strong,
> Eighteen million hearts behind us,
> Eighteen million minds to guide us,
> Eighteen million lives to bind us
> To our country and her flag."

On the altar of the nation we placed our lives and honor and all we possessed and though we are only 18% of the whole population what percentage did we give?

While certain groups were boasting they were 100 percenters Catholics were proving that they were 200% patriotic. Catholic eloquence in war is the eloquence of blood and in peace the eloquence of work. They attend to their business. On September 17, 1923, Mr. Edwin Denby, the Secretary of the United States Navy said: "I found that more than 45 per cent of the enlisted men were Catholic (over 200 per cent patriotic). And this is a grand tribute to the teaching of the fine old Church that it instills in the minds of the young a deep and loving patriotism that does not balk at the sacrifices of one's own life in the Nation's honor. Our

Lord says of such patriotism: "Greater love than this no man hath." [12]

In the terrible years of the greatest war which brought Catholic soldiers, priests, bishops, archbishops and cardinals into deadly conflict one against the other, what was the attitude of the Common Father of all: the Pope? Let the Pope himself answer: "Three things I shall have in view: To preserve perfect neutrality. To do all the good possible to all nations as charity dictates. To omit nothing that lies in my power to hasten the day of peace." The Vatican was Noah's Ark politically and spiritually, floating on the raging flood. As Noah kept company with all manner of animals, the Pope kept company with all manner of nations. His only ambassador was the dove. The New York American has been quoted as saying of him: "No single figure ever had more influence on our world during the anxious years of the war than Benedict XV." "The cell of Benedict XV," said another American editor, "was the only sane spot in the mind of a war-mad world."

The stability of the Vatican has been and is the marvel of all her enemies. She is like the house of which Christ speaks: "and the rain fell, and the floods came and the winds blew and they beat upon that house and it fell not, for it was founded on a rock." [13] How many more are the years of the

[12] John XV. 13.
[13] Matthew VII. 25.

United States government? God alone knows! But we know that the same laws which created her alone can preserve her. Without the Church the principles on which our Republic rests would never have been devised, liberty would not have been born. The source of our democratic institutions is the gospel entrusted by Christ to His Church for all nations and every creature to the end of time. In all her fundamental principles of government and discipline she is as nearly a copy of the Church, as far as any human institution can ever be a copy of the Divine.

What is the official attitude of those two institutions toward each other: ROME and WASHINGTON—POPE and PRESIDENT? We will let Pope Leo XIII. describe it:

"America seems destined for greater things; the Catholic Church should not only share in, but help bring about this greatness. We deem it right and proper that she should, by availing herself of the opportunity daily presented to her, keep equal step with the Republic in the march of improvement, at the same time striving to the utmost, by her virtue and her institutions, to aid the rapid growth of the States."

"In a free State, unless justice be generally cultivated, unless the people be repeatedly and diligently urged to observe the precepts and laws of the Gospel, liberty itself may be pernicious. Let those of the clergy, therefore, who are occupied in the instruction of the multitude, treat plainly of this topic of the duties of citizens, so that all may understand and feel the necessity, in political life, of conscientiousness, self-restraint, and integrity; for that cannot be lawful in public which is unlawful in private affairs."

"Without morality the State cannot endure—a truth which that illustrious citizen of yours (Washington), with a keenness of insight worthy of his genius and statesmanship, perceived and proclaimed. But the best and strongest support of morality is religion. . . . Now what is the Church other than a legitimate society, founded by the will and ordinance of Jesus Christ, for the preservation of morality and defence of religion."

What is the official attitude of Washington toward Rome, what is the attitude of the President toward the Pope? The President of the United States visited the Pope the only time that an American President had a chance to do so. The Holy Father's Peace proposals were addressed to every nation in the world even though many had no official representatives at the Vatican—but particularly to the United States. President Wilson's Fourteen Points contained nearly all the principles insisted on as a basis of peace by Benedict XV: "Moral right must be substituted for the material force of arms." And when the President visited the Pope in 1918, the Holy Father made an impassioned speech on the President's efforts for World Peace. Again, on the occasion of the Eucharistic Congress at Chicago, President Coolidge sent to the Governors of the Universal Church the message of the United States Government through our Secretary of Labor the Hon. James J. Davis:

"I have the very great honor of being able to bring to you the greetings of the President of the United States, and I bid you a hearty welcome to this Republic.

"When a million souls from all parts of the world leave their homes and vocations behind them for the purpose of making a pilgrimage of the extraordinary character which is now being witnessed in this city, it is proof, if proof be needed, that religion is neither dead nor moribund in the heart of man. The zeal that has brought you to this city on Lake Michigan's shore is comparable to that which inspired the knights of old who roamed far and wide in search of the Holy Grail, and made sacrifices of no mean order, to rescue the Holy Sepulchre from the Saracen.

"We often hear it said in America that the present age is one of unbridled materialism and worldliness. This gathering is a demonstration that the light of faith that burned so bright in the Middle Ages, is still burning with no diminution of its lustre. The faith that built the wonderful cathedrals of Europe and of the medieval universities which instructed the old and middle-aged as well as the young, the faith that inspired St. Francis and Dante, and made the thirteenth century so illustrious in the annals of mankind, is no less vital now than it was in those far off days.

"We are not oblivious in America of the spiritual side of existence. America was settled by men to whom spiritual things meant more than the things of purely material import. The Puritans who founded Massachusetts in the north, and the Catholics under Lord Baltimore who founded Maryland in the South, came to the new world that they might be permitted to worship God in accordance with their own conscience. America was founded by men who wished to see the will of God prevail in the world, and a religious people Americans have been ever since the days of the early settlements.

"It gives me great pleasure, in addressing this Catholic audience, to call attention to the fact that the members of your communion who settled in Maryland share with Roger Williams, the founder of Rhode Island and Providence plantations, in the honor of being the first American settlers to establish the principles of religious toleration. The Catholics of Maryland respected the conscience of all men and women in the province. They allowed the men and women of the various Protestant persuasions the same liberty that they asked for themselves. The student of history of religious freedom in America knows that in according toleration to all faiths, the Catholics of America, in the one original colony that was settled by them, built a monument to the great cause of religious freedom more enduring than one of bronze or marble.

"Catholics have reason to be proud of the growth of their faith in America. From humble beginnings the Church has grown by leaps and bounds until today it has nearly nineteen million communicants. Many of the leading citizens of our country are of your faith. They are graduates of our universities. They are to be found in editorial chairs; they are leaders in the arts and sciences; many are illustrious men of letters; they have taken an eminent rank in the profession and in business. Catholics are found in our halls of legislation and upon the bench. Two of their number, have been Chief Justices of the Supreme Court. On every field of battle in which America has engaged they have shed their blood in behalf of the land of their birth, or the land of their adoption, and on more than one hotly contested field a Catholic general has led the American arms. The patriotism of our Catholic citizens is not open to dispute. If there is any prejudice against Catholics in America, it comes from persons who make a specialty of prejudice, and like all other countries, we have a few who do.

"So far as the bulk of our people are concerned their minds are by nature tolerant of all that is tolerant. America has developed a neighborly spirit, in which all men and women who breathe a spirit of peace and good-will feel themselves at home. We have no quarrel with any man's religion; and any nation that refuses to grant freedom of worship is a nation that must realize sooner or later that it has made the profoundest of mistakes.

"There are elements among us, as in other lands, which are so dissatisfied with life, or rather, with the life that they know from experience that they desire to destroy our American institutions. These advocates of revolution are men who abhor all religion, and believe in neither God nor the life eternal. They are materialists against whom all who believe in the validity of spiritual ideals must set a face of flint. The Catholic Church has stood like a wall of adamant against the vicious revolutionary procedures of this class, which are urged ostensibly in behalf of labor, but which really owe their origin in the will of a few to power. Whatever a man's religious faith may be, if he have one, he can have no intellectual commerce with this type of revolutionist.

"Allow me to congratulate you heartily on the great success of this international Eucharistic Congress. Nothing like it in the way of purely religious celebration has ever been seen in America before, and its influence is destined to be profound. It was on your part a great spiritual adventure. I presume that the majority of these who have come from foreign lands are viewing America for the first time, and I trust that when you return to your homes, it will be to carry as pleasing a recollection of the people of the New World as we shall be certain to entertain of you. Prejudice dies on acquaintance, and is succeeded by good will. There is a good story told of Charles Lamb, the gentle and whimsical English essayist, that he was once heard expressing his hatred of somebody or other whom he did not even know, and was rebuked by his interlocutor on the ground that he had no right to hate a man if he did not know him. 'Why!' exclaimed Lamb, 'How could I hate him if I knew him?' To know one another is usually to like one another. Are we not all human?

"You have come to us as the representatives of the Church which has the greatest number of communicants who bear the Christian name. It was one of your faith who discovered the New World, and many of you have come from across the seas to rediscover it. As I have said, your Church has grown greatly in America, and it is still growing. Your influence in America is not confined to those of your own communion. Catholic authors are widely read among us, irrespective of denominational lines, and Catholic hymns are sung in all of our places of worship. The lives of your Saints are honored everywhere. The narrow prejudice and the intolerance of another day have vanished like the mist before the morning sun. You have found, and I hope you will always find in America—no matter what condition may prevail in other sections of this hemisphere—the freedom which you require to teach your faith to young and old and to be missionaries to us all.

"Again I bid you welcome to this Republic. I cannot conclude without a word of personal tribute to your host, who is not only universally respected and admired in this country, but greatly beloved by all who know him. He is in addition to being a great churchman, a wonderful business executive. It is my signal privilege on this occasion to be able to greet our beloved citizen, His Eminence George Cardinal Mundelein."

These facts amply demonstrate the happy relations that exist between the Pope and President, the Vatican and Washington. But in the eyes of Catholics who comes first? Rome or Washington, Pope or President? There is no first and there is no second. Each is first in his own sphere, in his own domain, in his own house. If there were any difficulty about giving allegiance to the Pope in spiritual matters and allegiance to the President in civil matters, Christ would not have commanded it when He said: "Render therefore to Cæsar the things that are Cæsar's; and to God, the things that are God's!" Give to the President what belongs to the President; and give to the Pope what belongs to the Pope. This principle is true and fixed for always by God the Author of Truth. Does the Catholic Church in the United States reconcile its principles and teachings to this truth? Read the Church's official teaching:

In 1837, the Catholic archbishops and bishops of the United States assembled in the Third Provincial Council of Baltimore, published the following declarations: "We owe civil and political allegiance to the several states in which we live and also to our general government. When we acknowledge the spiritual and ecclesiastical supremacy of the chief bishop of our Universal Church, the Pope, we do not thereby detract from the allegiance to which our temporal governments are plainly entitled and which we cheerfully give; nor do we acknowledge any civil or political supremacy, or power over us in any foreign potentate, even the chief pastor of our Church."

Again in 1852 the Catholic archbishops and bishops of our country assembled in the First Plenary Council of Baltimore, addressed those words to the Catholics of our country: "Attachment to the civil institutions under which you live has ever marked your conduct as citizens. We cannot, however, deem it altogether unnecessary to exhort you ever to discharge your civil duties from the higher motives which religion suggests. Obey the public authorities, not only for wrath, but for conscience sake. Show your attachment to the institutions of our beloved country by prompt compliance with all their requirements, and by the cautious jealousy with which you guard against the least deviation from the rules which they prescribe for the maintenance of public order and private rights."

Again, in 1884, the Catholic archbishops of our country assembled in the Third Plenary Council of Baltimore, made this declaration: "We repudiate the assertion that we need to lay aside any of our devotedness to our Church to be true Americans; that we need to abate any of our love for our country's principles and institutions to be faithful Catholics. We believe that our country's heroes were the instruments of God in establishing this home of freedom; to both the Almighty and to His instruments in the work, we look with grateful reverence, and to maintain the inheritance of freedom which they have left us should it ever be imperiled, our Catholic citizens will be found to stand forward as one man ready to pledge anew their lives, their fortunes, and their sacred honor."

In his Letter addressed to the Catholics of America in 1895 Pope Leo XIII said: "All men will agree that America seems destined for great things. The Catholic Church should not only share in, but should help to bring about this prospective greatness. She should keep equal step with the Republic in the march of improvement, striving to the utmost by her virtue and her institutions to aid in the rapid growth of the States . . . ever keeping before the minds of the people the enactments of the Councils of Baltimore, particularly those which inculcate the observance of the laws of the Republic."

Here you have, kind reader, before your eyes the official manner in which the Catholic Church reconciles her teachings with American Constitutional principles. From these series of comparisons and parallels thus far instituted in this book it is evident in fact that our American Government is not modeled on paganism, Mahomedanism or any of the Protestantisms; but is patterned in all her essentials on the Church. The antitype of every department is in the Church. The United States is a daughter of the Catholic Church.

IX

CROSS AND FLAG

"Lift high the Cross, unfurl the flag,
   May they forever stand
  United in our heart and hopes:
   God and our native land."

Selected.

GOD's Universal Kingdom was foretold hundreds of years before it became a visible fact under Christ the King. Daniel the prophet makes no apologies when he says that Christ's Kingdom shall consume all others. Itself shall not be destroyed but shall endure forever.

Lest politicians should misunderstand the nature of this Kingdom, Christ the King reassured one of them: "My Kingdom is not of this world." [1] His Kingdom is here on the earth but is not of earth in its origin. It is upheld by the pillars of truth, justice, charity and love! It has nothing to do with purely earthly affairs. It knows no national or material boundaries. It cannot stop to consider racial prejudices, social afflictions or capitalistic organizations. The Church has nothing to do with the sale or barter of foods and chattels, the construction of highways,

[1] John XVIII. 36.

waterways or railroads. She has no commission to
police towns or cities, or summon the nation to arms.
If, however, in carrying out these civil and political
functions, the State shall violate the Commandments
of God, the Church cannot be silent. She must pro-
claim the Law of God. Republics, Democracies,
Empires, Leagues and Leaders, Kings, Kaisers and
Caliphs, shall pass away but the Commandments
never.

God will not compromise with states or statesmen. Not man but God decides the fate of men and
nations. "Christ being the holiest among the mighty
and the mightiest among the holy, has lifted empires off their hinges, has turned the stream of centuries out of its channel and still governs the ages." [2]
If Christ has set up His Universal Kingdom on earth
and if all men are equal before God, that Kingdom
must be the same everywhere and forever.

Americans possess wonderful inventive genius but
if they must have an American Church they must
invent an American God. If God chose to operate
His Universal Kingdom through the agency of a society called the Church, what have we to do or to
say about it? Can we, by making speeches in the
Senate or by raising an army, do away with God?
Can we by a majority vote, put Him out of the
country as a foreigner? Can we tell Him that He has
no right to dictate to us how we must serve Him?

God is the center of all that was, is or shall be.

[2] Richter.

God is love! Christian civilization centers everything
in God. All other forms make individuals the center.
It is not for man to tell others what to believe or do.
God and not man creates truth. Now if Catholicity
be Christianity, and if Christianity be from God, why
should Americans wish to reject it? If in 1776 we
needed a new government, does it follow that we
needed a new God and a new religion? How shall
we test the origin of any work or any religion? In
the Fifth Chapter of the Acts of the Apostles we
read:

"If this Council or this work be of men; it will come to
naught. But if it be of God you cannot overthrow it; lest
perhaps you be found even to fight against God." (Acts V.
38-39).

Who wants to fight against God or banish Him
into eternal exile? If America is a daughter of the
Catholic Church, why should the daughter desire
to get rid of the mother? Why should the one be in
conflict with the other? Why is the Catholic Church
in the United States a sign to be contradicted? Turn
back a page of history and read the answer. Christ
commanded all men to do penance, to chastise themselves, to deny themselves, to practice humility, putting self last and others first, to take up the Cross,
to love their enemies and to do good to those who
hate and persecute them. Such a program seemed
foolish, absurd and superstitious to intelligent
men. "A Cross," they cried, "take away that hideous

thing!" This is not all. Christ set this cross over all
nations, and over the whole world: "In this Sign
thou shalt conquer." The Apostles themselves accepted the cross but wanted to appropriate it for
one people and one nation only: the Jewish race.
They were willing to admit the Gentiles to membership in the Church, provided that they first became
Jews. At this crisis it was revealed to Peter, the
Supreme Pontiff, that the Church ought not to be a
Jewish community; that Gentiles may be Christians
without being Jews, that the Church is a Divine international society, where all shall meet without
distinctions of rite or race, the Jew and the Gentile,
the slave and the master, the poor and the rich.
Such a program wounded the patriotic feelings of
the Jews, and many of them from that day to this
have wept bitter tears that God broke down the
barriers of their State, and invited all nations and
every creature into the fold of the Church. This
tearing down of the lines of nationality, brought
the Church into conflict with the strongest sentiments of man's nature. National pride within reason stimulates national progress. Carried to excess
it is the root of many social evils. Coupled with
temporal success it breeds contempt for everything
foreign. To cure this contempt for one's neighbor,
our Lord invented an international nation in which
all men may be brothers in Christ: a universal
democracy wherein the first may be last and the last
may be first.

What, then, are the nations to do about this "kill-joy religion," enemy of man's luxuries, pleasures and revels; this independent international society with a Supreme Pontiff commanding obedience in the name of the World's Maker; bringing a warning to high and low, "Unless you do penance you shall all likewise perish?" [3] The Jewish politicians could never accept such an institution as this. They must therefore wage war on her. To start a war a reason must be invented. Money and an army must be raised. The deepest passions must be aroused. National pride must be appealed to. The propaganda is started. The Founder of this kill-joy religion is disloyal. We find Him stirring up rebellion. The State is in danger. He and His followers are the enemies of the human race. They are plotting the downfall of the government. Under the plea of religion they are setting up a political machine whose principles are in conflict with the State. No member of such a society can be trusted with public office. Let us strike down the Head and throw the followers to the lions.

The calumnies worked. The people believed every word of it. Started a religious war which lasted three hundred years. One million Christians were sacrificed to the jealousy of the State. Go through the long annals of history century by century, and these same methods and calumnies are rehearsed. The destinies of the Founder must, as He repeatedly de-

[3] Luke XIII. 3, 5.

clared, be found in the Church which He established
and identified with Himself.

Then came the religious revolution of the 16th
century: civil war in the spiritual Kingdom of Christ.
Several states seceded from the Union of Christendom. In the Universal Church, by her Divine Constitution, all nations had an equal place. If they
broke away and subjected themselves to civil authority, becoming a department of the state, they did so
by rebellion. If they now return, they can do so only
by submission to the Universal and Spiritual Federa-
tion of the Kingdom of Christ. The Universal Apostolic Church is older than the oldest Christian nation, since she created them all.

To give a reason to the world and to their followers for rebellion, they simply repeated the old
calumnies which worked so well against the early
Christians. It was decreed that everything Catholic
stands for what is vile, idolatrous, superstitious,
bloody, unholy and unpatriotic. And lo! it was ac-
complished. There began the Protestant tradition
which was carefully handed down from father to
son, and from mother to daughter, from Sunday
School to High School to University, to magazine
and novel and history, till it became bone of their
bone and flesh of their flesh.

Let me illustrate by one story in a thousand the
effect of this Protestant tradition on men's minds:

"It is hard nowadays to realize the extent and the strength
of this Protestant tradition against the Pope. You know

that the calendar, or our method of reckoning time, is a very complicated arrangement. As the sun in its course round the earth consumes a fraction more than three hundred and sixty-five days, our reckoning of three hundred and sixty-five days to the year is not accurate. As the fraction is very small it was not noticed at first, but in the course of centuries it became so great that it amounted to more than a week. In 1582 Pope Gregory XIII. reformed the calendar, and introduced the system which obtains among us to-day. The Catholic countries adopted the change; but the Protestant nations, which are, according to their own notions, in the van of progress, clung to the antiquated calendar, because the new style was the work of a Pope. England did not come into line until 1751. By that time the error had amounted to eleven days, and it was necessary to suppress them, nominally, in September, 1752. The pious British Protestants were, in the first place, scandalized that a Protestant government should sanction a Popish invention, and, in the second place, they were convinced that in some way or other the Pope had got hold of the missing days and was applying them to his own nefarious purposes. The mob rose in its wrath, surrounded the ministers' houses, and split the air with the demand, 'Give us back our eleven days.' " [4]

Such prejudice and ignorance is not dissolved in a day. In truth the outcroppings of this religious affliction affected the social and civil holdings of mankind. In consequence, these European governments failed miserably to bring peace or happiness to their subjects at home.

But God never intended that the hates and fears

[4] Rev. P. C. Yorke: "Ghosts of Bigotry," p. 214.

of the Old World should take root in the New. During all those terrible centuries of tears and blood, while the race was being chastised and civilized, Providence was preparing a home in the New World "where strangers from afar may come and breathe the air of liberty." Bancroft says that: "Lord Baltimore (the Catholic) formed in Maryland the first home of religious freedom in the world." But along with the first settlers who moved into that part of the New World which has become the United States came all the religious and political differences of the Old World. It is worthy of note, that any success they scored in bringing about religious peace, was in so far as the enactments of civil and criminal laws could restrain physical violence.

By a God-given courage and wisdom our political forefathers—Protestant, Catholic, non-Catholic, patterned the grandest system of political unity ever made by man. How they did so we have studied in other pages. Their desire was to enact laws for the establishment, and to lay the corner stone of a Nation which would forever be free from religious persecution. Their hopes were that every man and woman would enjoy fully the privileges of worshiping God in such a way as would best satisfy spiritual hunger.

While in a large sense this ideal has been maintained, we cannot overlook the sad and unfortunate religious discussions and disputes that have played such a prominent part in the growth of our country.

While the political oneness of the Nation has been upheld and the highest standards of morality instituted, Protestantism has been divided and subdivided many times and the Catholic Church alone has been able to preserve her unity. The unity of the Catholic Church in the United States and the unity of our Government constitute one more unique parallel.

Because of this unity of authority, the one spiritual, the other political, in the Catholic Church and in the United States Government, both institutions in their sphere have achieved phenomenal success. In striking contrast to the political oneness of our Government, and the spiritual unity of the Catholic Church, stands Protestantism, the greatest example of religious disunity the world has ever beheld.

We have reviewed the efforts of our Government to maintain civil unity in peace and war. But remember that the Fathers of the Church battled against spiritual heresies and schisms, by which the forces of evil attempted to dismember the spiritual body of the Universal Church. We ought never forget that the United States is a new and very young country. It is only a corner of the universal battlefield upon which are being fought out the issues of religious unrest. The Mother Church never ceases in her efforts to bring about unity among the scattered armies of the Cross.

When the war of the Southern States ended, peace was not brought about by writing a new constitution for all the states, or by compromising between the

old Constitution and the new one of the confeder-
ated rebellious states. It was brought about by a
common acknowledgment of the wisdom and per-
fection of the old Constitution, and by complete
submission to the President. The Constitution of
the Church and the Law of Christ were revealed
to us by Holy Scripture and the early Fathers. Their
writings and teachings are as old as the New Testament and are in harmony with it. A return to the
original Constitution is the answer to all questions
pertaining to a final settlement of this disunity.

In the first centuries Christ was on trial before
the pagan world and men judged Him by the unity
of His followers: "See how these Christians love
one another." Today about 400 Christian sects are
asking the millions of pagans and heathens and un-
believers to accept Christ, on the testimony of more
than 400 contradictory witnesses. And the pagan
world in mockery answers: "You ask us to consider
Christianity, and before our eyes you meet in solemn
session to disagree on everything except His Name.
Your sects have given up religion and have entered
politics, and if you had your way you would dismember the unity of the Constitution as you did the Unity
of the Church."

Anarchy in religion is frequently followed by
anarchy in politics. It would not be difficult to prove
this from history. That all is not serene within the
camp I leave Mr. Frederick Haskin of Washington,
D. C., to say:

"There are more than a thousand publications in the country at this time which are either openly or covertly advocating the forcible overthrow of our Government.

"Millions of pamphlets carrying distorted and malicious information are in circulation, and thousands of speakers are spreading the poisonous doctrine of discontent." [5]

This statement evokes many questions: For example; it might be asked, from which group—Protestant, Catholic or non-Catholic—are the malcontents recruited? Our worst enemies cannot point to a single Catholic publication inciting to violence or advocating the overthrow of our Government. Have you ever heard of a Catholic Bolshevism, Red-Radicalism or Communism? Who ever heard of a Catholic society like the Know-Nothings, A. P. A. or K. K. K. organizations operating to deprive particular groups of citizens of the blessings promised by the Constitution of the United States? Show me a single Catholic publication "which carries malicious information or seeks to spread the poisonous doctrine of discontent." There is no Catholic Blue Law organization seeking to close our golf links on Sundays, our newsstands and ice cream fountains. On the contrary, and in striking contrast, the obedience of the Catholic to every Constitutional Commandment is proverbial. The patriotism of the Catholic is the patriotism of John Adams: "To swim or

[5] Frederick J. Haskin: "The Biggest Business in the World," p. 4.

sink, live or die, survive or perish with my country is my unalterable determination."

The greatest anachronism in America today is the man living in the 20th century and walking, thinking and seeing in the 16th. He judges people not by what they are in themselves, not by what they do and say, but by what their ancestors did and said 400 years ago. And you know that Jews, Catholics and Protestants have had some ancestors who were a disgrace to humanity. Why judge a family by the worst type? If we start digging up the bones of our ancestors, dig them all up, the good and bad, Catholic and Protestant, saint and sinner, and then we will discover that there was nothing in any of them save corruption, without charity and love.

Why not let the dead rest? Trouble not their bones, but follow the practical philosophy of the ancients: "Say nothing of the dead, save what is good;" and when we judge the living it would be well to recall the philosophy of Robert Burns: "a man's a man for a' that."

In the February, 1928, number of THE CATHOLIC WORLD published by the Paulist Fathers at 411 West 59th Street, New York City, there appeared the following comment by its famous editor, Father Gillis:

"I am constantly stumbling upon addenda to the editorial on Governor Smith's chances for the presidency, published in these columns last June. Some readers may remember this sentence: 'But mark my word, if "Al" Smith runs for president, he will be opposed not with his record in New York State, but with the record of Cesare Borgia in Italy, not on the ground of what has happened in this State since Smith took the reins of government in 1919, but on what happened in Spain, or Italy, or England, or France, two hundred, or three hundred, or a thousand years ago. We shall hear about the Massacre of St. Bartholomew's Day, as if Governor Smith had murdered Hugenots with his own hands; we shall hear of the Spanish Inquisition as if Governor Smith were Torquemada reincarnate.' Again, in December, 1927, I referred to the fulfillment of that prophecy in the establishment on Broadway, New York, of an exhibition of paintings of the Spanish Inquisition with the disingenuous advertisement, 'No! These paintings are not a part of a political plot against Governor Smith.' Now, in the New York World of the third of January there appeared a letter, signed 'Masonic Philosopher,' which comes as a kind of corollary to my remarks. The writer says:

" 'I am a Mason. I joined the great order thirty years ago. I am loyal to its precepts and constitution. I was born and raised a Protestant. By the road of life I have picked up and stored away bits of philosophy.

" 'Yesterday on Broadway my eye was caught by something in a window. It was a colored photograph of an oil painting depicting a terrible scene from the Spanish Inquisition. This was an advertisement of a collection of nineteen paintings illustrating the fearful persecutions of that period. The entire collection was on exhibition in the shop beyond the window.

" 'I paid the admission fee and went into the shop. I walked slowly around the room looking at pictures of men and women marching to the stake and tortured in the fires.

The whole thing was dreadful. It was dreadful because the pictures told so much that was true. Let us not blink authentic revealments of history.

" 'But this is what I am now driving at: I wanted another and further row of paintings hung in that room, parallel to the row representing the Catholic cruelties in Spain. In this other and further row I wanted a picture of John Calvin, the protagonist of Presbyterianism, condemning Servetus, the Unitarian, to death by fire, and a companion picture of the flames licking that martyr's face, there in the public square at Geneva. I wanted a collection of pictures showing Anglicans burning Catholics and Anabaptists at Smithfield in England. I wanted a picture showing the Calvinistic Knox in Scotland preaching Queen Mary to the scaffold. I wanted a group of pictures representing Scotch Presbyterians and Massachusetts Puritans torturing squirming and screaming witches. I even wished for a picture of John Scopes paying his fine and losing his job at Dayton in Tennessee.

" 'We hate half-truths. Let the whole record appear. Let another and a further line of pictures parallel the line already hanging in that exhibition on Broadway. Let the people see both. Much of truth lies in both.

" 'It is a pity to have men's minds drawn back to the consuming passions and prejudices of an age dead beyond recall. In this advanced stage of the world the true Catholic and the true Protestant deep down in their hearts are murmuring to one another: "Forgive me for what I was and accept me for what I am."

" 'Nobody imagines that it would be possible now, at Geneva, or at Smithfield, or at Edinburgh, or at Salem, or at any other spot on the globe, to induce the most devout

Calvinist or Anglican or Puritan even to warm the back of a Catholic's hand or the tip of an Anabaptist's finger or the end of a Voodoo's toe with a lighted cigaret. Not in these days and time. By like token it is unthinkable that the modern Catholic would so much as strike a match on the seat of his pants to singe even one small, wild hair on the back of a modern Protestant's neck.

" 'So why call up old, dead stuff from a dim age? But if we must call up this stuff, let us call it all up. Then let us look at it all through tears of toleration and understanding.' "

If this book is anything it is an appeal to all citizenry to refill their hearts with respect for the Fathers of our Country, to keep the light of Truth burning in the temple of the Nation at the shrine of religious liberty and constituted authority. At this turning point in the tide of times, at this crisis in the world when the old institutions are being replaced by the new, the Church remains as ever, the greatest fact in the world, a fact which we may try to get around by calumny and caricature, yet cannot get over:

"As some tall cliff that lifts its awful form,
Swells from the vale, and midway leaves the storm.
Though 'round its breast the rolling clouds are spread,
Eternal sunshine settles on its head." [6]

The convulsions of 1914 have rocked Christian nations to their foundation. The next war, we are told, will wipe out whole nations in a day or two.

[6] Goldsmith: "Deserted Village."

May it not be better for the nations of the world to
bring religion and justice and charity to the same
standard of efficiency as science, than to pursue science to their own destruction? The Catholic Church
is best equipped to answer all the problems of the
nations; to her they are not new. A great writer has
said: "The Catholic Church held the four corners of
the world in place, while it trembled from the shock
of a World War." Our own national reputation is
at stake. We lead the world in crime and in disre-
spect for law and moral discipline. The wealthier we
grow the worse we become; and Goldsmith tells us
whither this leads:

> "Ill fares the land, to hastening ills a prey,
>   Where wealth accumulates, and men decay."

Lord Byron has well said that what happened to
others may happen to us:

> "This is the moral of all human tales
> 'Tis the same rehearsal of the past,
>   First freedom, then glory and when this fails
> Wealth, corruption, barbarism at last,
> And history with all her volumes vast
>   Hath but one page."

Religion alone can save us. It requires a moral and
spiritual force to cope with a moral and spiritual
foe. It has become a proverb that the nation that
does not serve God will perish. The world is sick of

human theories, and leagues and conventions. The world wants a reality, a fact and a friend.

In his address in 1908 before the First American Catholic Missionary Congress, the Hon. Bourke Cockran said:

"The Catholic Faith, Catholic worship and Catholic fervor throughout the country must operate to stimulate the loyalty of American citizens; it cannot operate to weaken, but must always operate to support this government; it is the strongest force that can be enlisted in its defense—not merely is She the strongest force that can contribute to the safety of this Republic; She is the only force by which its safety can be completely assured.

"She cannot exercise any of her functions without yielding enormous benefit to the State. Since She cannot administer a Sacrament from Her altars, teach a lesson from Her pulpits, impose a penance or enjoin an act of reparation in the confessional without laboring effectively to strengthen the government and promote the general welfare, the Church and the State are interdependent. The State no longer supports the Church and can never be permitted to support Her, but the Church must always support the State."

She is a fact and a friend. Her mission and aim is to bring to the World a blessing and a balm: "The Peace of Christ in the reign of Christ the King." We who trust in God welcome Him. Have we not already experienced His love? He makes the cup of our prosperity run over with every blessing. He has caused our "harvests to wave, our cities to rise" and to live in, "gave us earth's loveliest paradise"—America.

Jews, Catholics and Protestants stand shoulder to shoulder. They stand against the enemies within the Nation—the enemies of law and order and constituted authority. In eloquent words our own American poet, William Cullen Bryant, bids us take courage:

> "Truth crushed to earth will rise again,
> The Eternal years of God are hers.
> While error wounded writhes in pain
> And dies amid her worshipers."

God gave us minds to know. He gave us hearts to love. The better we know each other, the more we will love each other. What a glorious spectacle we were to all the world in the days of trial; the days of a World War: 114,000,000 [7] hearts united in prayer to the God who brought victory to our arms! Once again let us unite that this Nation under God may have a new birth to freedom. Let us consecrate ourselves anew to Christ our King:

We, sons and daughters of America, salute Thee, our Captain and our King! We pledge to Thee our lives, our honor, and all that we are; and declare that wherever Thy Cross and our Flag shall lead us, even though it be to the battlefield or to Calvary, there too with the help of Thy Love shall we always be found.

[7] The Census Bureau estimates that the population of the United States will be 120,013,000 next July.

SUPPLEMENTARY NOTE

The manuscript of this work was completed and was in the hands of the publishers when the following "inside" story of one of the world's greatest statesmen appeared, it seems, for the first time for public eyes. It was printed in the New York *World* March 10, 1928.

MR. ROOSEVELT UPON RELIGIOUS FREEDOM

To the Editor of the World:

Recently I came into possession of a letter written by President Roosevelt when he was in the White House to the Rev. John B. Worrall, a Presbyterian minister in Kansas City, who had protested against the official reception given by the President to Cardinal Satolli.

Now that it seems likely that we shall have a Catholic President, I think the attitude of President Roosevelt on this subject is of peculiar public interest. Furthermore, I think that his sane, intelligent and patriotic words might well be published at this time when there is so much dissension along these lines. So far as I know, the letter has not been published before, although I am not sure on that point.

GEO. GORDON BATTLE.

New York, March 7.

MR. ROOSEVELT'S LETTER
(COPY)

WHITE HOUSE,
Washington, Aug. 1, 1904.

(Personal)

My dear Sir:

I have your letter of the 29th instant. What I write you is personal and not for publication, for I do not regard it as seemly or proper to enter into a discussion which may give rise to anything like sectarian bitterness. Last winter I received a delegation of visiting Welsh Methodist clergymen at the White House. I received a delegation of visiting Congregationalist ministers from England at the White House. I received a delegation of Scotch Presbyterians at the White House and had two of their number to dinner. I received a delegation of Lutheran ministers from Germany. I received a delegation of Baptists from Australia at the White House. Next September the Archbishop of Canterbury is coming here and I shall have him to dine at the White House. I received Cardinal Satolli at the White House just exactly as I received the Methodists, the Presbyterians, the Baptists, the Lutherans, &c. I am President of all the people, I shall not discriminate for or against a man because he is a Catholic or because he is a Protestant, and Catholic or Protestant ecclesiastics who come here and who are men of reputable character will be received by me with the same courtsey. Surely you must agree with this, and I feel I shall have your sympathy with my attitude when I state that I desire to handle myself toward Catholics exactly as I should wish a Catholic President to handle himself toward Protestants— in other words, as I think an American President should behave toward all honest men of any creed.

Sincerely yours,

THEODORE ROOSEVELT.

For The Rectory—The Pulpit—The Home—The Office—The School
and College

The best selling Ethics in America—used in leading Universi-
ties, Colleges, Academies, Schools of Sociology, and
by individual Professors and Teachers

—*bigotry!* —its cause, its curse—Ignorance
—its Cure? Knowledge

No man or woman is more independent in thought and action than a *practical* Catholic.

No man or woman is better equipped to defend in thought, word and action the
Constitution of their country than a *practical* Catholic.

All prejudice, all bigotry, is born of ignorance; and the ignorance of educated men
and women, thousands upon thousands of them Catholics, too, concerning Catholic
teaching, Catholic ethics, is amazing.

A book that every priest will gladly lend to educated Protestants—urge upon educated Catholic men and women, who in homes, clubs, offices and elsewhere glibly
discuss anything and everything from politics and stocks to scandals and sheer stock-
ings, but who become shrinking violets when their religion is attacked. Probably
nine in ten of them are helpless to enlighten their ignorant non-Catholic friends and all
because of their own crass ignorance of Catholic fundamentals.

How to Be a Practical Christian—a Practical Catholic via

THE BOOK OF RIGHT LIVING
CHRISTIAN ETHICS

By REV. J. ELLIOT ROSS, C.S.P., Ph.D.

Formerly Lecturer in Ethics to the Newman Club, University of Texas, now Chaplain
to Newman Club, Columbia University, New York

For the practical and moral instruction of students and of the general reader Fr. Ross
has doubtless produced the best book on Christian Ethics that has so far appeared in
the English language. Any intelligent person can read this book, not only with understanding and profit, but with entertainment and pleasure. It is not surprising that this
book is in such great demand in schools and in colleges as well as among those who
have finished their days at school.   CHAS. J. CALLAN, O.P.

The more I think of Ross's book, the more I feel that it should somehow be made
the textbook on Ethics in every Catholic college and school. JOHN J. WYNNE, S.J.

Business Men and Women—Officers and Directors of Corporations
—Bankers and Credit Men will find Doctor Ross's book an inspiration
for themselves and for those who work for them. They may use
The Book of Right Living to upbuild Manhood, Womanhood, Character
—Honesty. All Employees should have a copy of *The Book of Right
Living.* It will help them to think clearly, act clearly—get results.

PRICE, $3.50 NET, $3.65 POSTPAID

THE DEVIN-ADAIR COMPANY, *Publishers*
23 and 25 MADISON SQUARE NORTH   NEW YORK

A rose gets its color and fragrance from the root, and man his virtue from his childhood.

Austin O'Malley in KEYSTONES OF THOUGHT

INNOCENCE AND IGNORANCE

J. ELLIOT ROSS — M. S. GILLET

"Innocence and Ignorance" is the best discussion of both sides of sex-instruction I have seen; rather, it is the only examination of that grave and dangerous matter worth reading. This book should be in the hand of every parent and teacher.
(Signed) *Austin O'Malley, M.D., Ph.D., LL.D.*

The Book will prove valuable to pastors, parents and teachers, to all of whom the author's sanity not less than his spirituality cannot but commend itself.—*The Ave Maria*

Teachers and others who know the devious ways by which the young often come to the knowledge of things sexual will welcome "Innocence and Ignorance." We have here no mere manual of sex enlightenment but rather an accurate analysis of the various methods that have been advanced for dealing with this delicate problem.—
America

The whole work, in fact, is addressed first of all to parents. The safety of the children lies in their hands. They show strikingly how easy it is for the parent who keeps and fosters the confidence of his children, to lead them safely through the dark waters of nature's upheaval; how helpless the task of that parent who loses hold of his children's hearts. The value of such a book to educators and confessors is very great.—*The Catholic World*

FATHER, MOTHER, TEACHER, CONFESSOR—and all men and women who look forward to marriage and parenthood should read and reread this truly interesting, instructive work. It will enable and encourage you to talk to children, to youth, to maturing adolescents and to adults on a matter more vital than life. Ninety-nine per cent of all sin, all crime is comprehended in the 6th, 7th, and 8th Commandments, and perhaps more than 90% of it is directly or remotely due to sex incentive. When your sons and daughters are from twelve to sixteen years of age take them to a good doctor. Insistently send them regularly to the Sacrament of Penance. It is the best of all recipes for preserving and transmitting mental, moral and physical health. Go with them. You have no right to ask your children to do what you don't do. The Confessional is today the only Court of Justice in this lawyer-throttled country for a square husband with a crooked wife. A Good Wife-Mother is God's masterpiece. The Devil's masterpiece is also a woman.

Price, $2.00 Net, and Postpaid

THE DEVIN-ADAIR COMPANY, *Publishers*

23 and 25 MADISON SQUARE NORTH   NEW YORK

Is Your Body a "Haunted House"?

A Catholic father, yielding to a son's wishes, sent his eighteen-year-old first-born to a leading "fashionable" University. Of course, there is a Catholic Club there—for Catholic students whose parents are prominent socially, professionally, commercially; prominent too in front pews, but how few of these Blue Book exclusives are ever seen enter a confessional! The young man, now in his junior year, recently wrote the following letter, which is authentic and reads verbatim:

"Father, you probably don't know just what courses your boy at —— University is taking. Stripped of their official titles, they are roughly: Plato and Aristotle, William James, 19th Century French literature, and finally a course in what amounts to Materialism; at least the man who gives it denies the existence of any form of immortal soul; or, as he puts it, denies that man is a "haunted house," and lectures to us on his proofs that mind or spirit of any sort does not exist, except when used as a synonym for brain or body."

Christ has long since been discarded by the world's leaders—blasphemously referred to as "only a Modernist Jew and of dubious sanity." Now "there is no God—no soul, no immortality." Our great Intellectuals have dropped mind, heart, and soul into the pelvis.

There is an epidemic of suicides in high school and college youths. Why not—with stuff like the above taught them orally or in the works of these pelvic philosophers!

WHAT IS FAITH?

By REV. CHARLES J. CALLAN, O.P.

Just lend it to your leading Catholic Mothers and Fathers — ask them to lend it in turn to their materialistic friends, Catholic and non-Catholic.

Price $1.90   Net and Postpaid

THE DEVIN-ADAIR COMPANY, *Publishers*

23 and 25 MADISON SQUARE NORTH   NEW YORK

—more than sixty editions of
THE LIGHT OF MEN
sold throughout the world

There isn't in print a book more interesting, inspiring—yes inspiriting, than THE LIGHT OF MEN.

It you are a Woman, of this rapid age, keep the book beside your bed, turn to it nightly and you will soon forget lipstick, rouge pot and cigarette as you gaze thoughtfully into the Mirror of Perfect Womanhood—the Mother of her own Divine Creator.

If you are a Man that rises only to the rustle of the dollar, read THE LIGHT OF MEN. It will bring you closer to the Christ who never entered a Banker's Club banquet to prate about Charity that is all oral—rarely active, and who when He died didn't have enough wealth to be host to a tramp.

THE LIGHT OF MEN
By M. REYNES MONLAUR (Crowned by the French Academy)

Read in "THE LIGHT OF MEN" the truly beautiful Prose Prelude to the Blessed Virgin. Read the entire work; read it to those you love—give it to them that they may read it all through life. Lend or give it to those who are dubious of the Divinity of Our Lord—or of the supernal merits of His Blessed Mother. After a wasted evening at the vile movies and plays from which you return less a Man, less a Woman, spend a few minutes with "THE LIGHT OF MEN" before retiring. It will sweeten your slumber and you will waken more a Man, more a Woman.

The "Light of Men" is the story of the most eventful week in the history of the world—a week that gave to the human race Christianity (Catholic, Protestant, Christian Science, etc., etc.) and its eternal pivots: the Eucharist—the Cross—the Mass.

Lend or Give "The Book of Right Living," "What is Faith?" "Innocence and Ignorance," to non-Catholic friends. These books one and all will please them—and you in results—for they are as foreign to "kitchen theology and drawing-room cant" as Heaven is to the Rogues' Gallery.

PRICE $1.90 NET — POSTPAID $2.00

THE DEVIN-ADAIR COMPANY, *Publishers*
23 and 25 MADISON SQUARE NORTH   NEW YORK

Date Due

JUL 30			
JUL 5 38			
FEB 24 39			
JAN 29 40			
FEB 19 40			
Ja 31 '41			
Ap 1 '41			
A 28 42			

Demco 293–5